STUDYING VS. LEARNING:

The Psychology of Student Success

Troy Dvorak

DEDICATIONS

Mom

The confidence I have, goals I set, and things I achieve all stem from your unwavering love and support. Your faith in me is a cornerstone of my career choices and desire to help others. As a woman, professional, and mother, you are an amazing role model. I am grateful for you and love you more than I can ever express.

Big Sister

The learning books you made me when I was a kid paid off! You helped me value learning, be a good student, and (hopefully) become a good teacher. Baby Brother loves his Big Sister.

My Students

Thank you for teaching me something new every day. I hope to do the same for you. For those of you who shared your opinion for the title of this book, I appreciate your input. Is this the title you voted for?

Gail O'Kane

Sharing your insights, expertise, and experiences as a leader at our college made this book so much better. For all your time, advice, feedback, and editing, thank you!

In Memoriam

With gratitude to John Heinrichs for his unwavering support of Minneapolis Community & Technical College students. He is missed.

TABLE OF CONTENTS

SECTION 1:
LEARNING HOW TO LEARN

ARE YOU LEARNING, OR JUST STUDYING?

Typical studying strategies are useless if you don't know how to think and how to learn.

Schools spend a lot of time and energy teaching information to students, but often without instruction on **how** to learn the information.[1] That's like giving you an unassembled car with no instructions on how to build it. You can know the names of all the parts and understand what they all do. You can know all the ways the car will be useful when it is built. But without knowing how to put it all together, the parts are useless.

In my experience, teachers give students a lot of advice about how to study. You know what I'm talking about, right? They tell you about studying skills such as re-reading, highlighting things you read, making flashcards, memorizing, summarizing, and doing practice questions. However, if you want to maximize your learning and success, you need quality **thinking skills, learning skills, and psychological skills** far more than you need studying tips.

Have you ever studied for a test, passed it (or better), and then two weeks later, realized you have forgotten most of it? I certainly had experiences like that when I was in school. That is a great example of how we can study but not learn very much. So, are you learning, or just studying?

In a perfect world, studying leads to learning. But as you can see, studying and learning are not necessarily the same thing. To learn, you must know **how to think**. Thinking skills are **not** the same as studying skills. Thinking skills will make your studying skills more effective.

Please consider this quotation: "Learning how to learn cannot be left to students. It must be taught."[2] Most students think about learning information in school. If you are doing well in high school, or if you are attending college, you probably don't think you need to learn how to learn. Some of you may be right.

Before you jump to that conclusion, consider this: A study in 1995 showed that 79 percent of students starting at a community college felt prepared for college-level work, but more than half left school with no degree two years later.[3] Data from a 2011 study showed that only 20 percent of students who enrolled in a two-year public college had graduated three years later.[4] Do you want to become part of these statistics? I'm confident your answer is, "No!"

Do not be discouraged by statistics like that. This book will help you develop thinking skills and psychological skills to succeed in high school, college, and your career. For example, having strong academic goals, motivation, confidence in your own abilities, and self-control will help you stay in school (i.e., persist) and graduate.[5,6,7] Those aren't studying skills. They are thinking and psychological skills that help you succeed.

I would be lying if I told you that hard work and good thinking skills will get all of you through to graduation and career success. There are many factors related to academic achievement. For example, many of my students have children and work part- or full-time. Others face significant hardships such as poverty and even homelessness.

Scholars and researchers have also looked at how intelligence is related to academic achievement (that is a huge topic and is not the focus of this book).[8] Many students get worried when they see the word intelligence. Some worry that they aren't smart enough to do well in school. If you are one of those students, there is a nice metaphor[9] that might set your mind at ease. Each of us is like a rubber band when it comes to intelligence. We come in different sizes. There is nothing we can do to change the size of the rubber band we happen to be. However, we are all capable of stretching a lot. This book will help you develop the skills and strategies that will allow you to...

S - T - R - E - T - C - H .

Being "smart" is helpful, but hard work, practice, persistence, and developing specific skills really matter. For example, one study found that report card grades were predicted more by self-control and homework completion than by IQ scores.[10] You need "skill, will, and self-regulation"[11] for learning and success. As for success in life, there is much research showing that emotional intelligence (i.e., recognizing, understanding, and managing emotions) can take you much further than IQ smarts.[12] You'll read about that in the psychological skills section of this book.

So, what are your thoughts about being a successful student? Is academic success about intelligence? Studying hard? Getting good grades? Just passing? Memorizing stuff? Getting a degree? What exactly does a successful student look like? Would you know a successful student if you saw one? Is that student staring back at you in the mirror?

If you want the student in the mirror to be successful, keep reading and I will help you develop thinking skills, learning skills, and psychological skills that will help you *stretch*!

YOUR LEARNING OBJECTIVES

Studying is what you do to pass a test.
Learning is what you do to be knowledgeable
and useful in the real world.

Graduating high school and enrolling in college represents a chance to dramatically improve your life. But even the greatest schools and teachers cannot guarantee your success. The only true guarantor of your success (or failure) is *you*. When you start college, the expectation is that you can organize and manage your own life. It is critical that you make effective decisions about studying and adapt to the expectations of your instructors and college.[1] Enrolling in college is a declaration of your willingness to do all the work. College expectations don't change if you lack skills or have too many other things to do.

"Academic-intellectual work is heavily cognitive, requiring combinations of knowledge and reasoning skills."[2] What does that mean? I'm glad you asked because I'm going to tell you. Earning a college degree is hard work. It requires a lot of effort, studying, concentration, and a stick-with-it attitude. You need to develop some skills (that many students don't know about) to keep up with the rigors of a college education. The first year of college is when you develop attitudes, approaches toward learning, and perceptions of yourself as a college student that can help (or hurt) you.[3]

Your Learning Objectives for This Book

The title of this book is *Studying vs. Learning.* I hope you already wondered what this means. Aren't studying and learning kind of the same thing? At a minimum the two are closely related, right? Don't you study to learn…learn by studying?

As a college instructor, I have seen a lot of students do poorly, *not* because they are stupid, but because they lack important thinking, learning, and psychological skills. They simply don't realize that studying and learning are not always the same. Studying is what you do to pass a test; learning is what you do to be knowledgeable and useful in the world.

When a class begins at my college, the instructor explains to students what the learning outcomes are. That means we tell you what you can expect to learn and know by the end of the semester. These are called learning objectives. They are important to you because they help you organize, understand, and remember **what** you are learning and **why** you are learning it.

With this book, *your learning objectives are:*

1. Learn about and develop thinking, learning, and psychological skills (the "<u>what</u>");

2. Understand <u>why</u> those skills and strategies are more important than basic studying strategies; and

3. Understand exactly <u>how</u> to learn in more effective ways.

The Thinking Skills

This book is going to help learn **how to think**. These thinking skills will make you a more effective student and serve you well in your career (and even your relationships, believe it or not). I call them the Psychological Keys to Student Success. They are:

1. Beliefs & Mindset
2. Attributions
3. Achievement Goals & Interest
4. Self-efficacy
5. Metacognition
6. Self-regulated Learning (SRL)
7. Avoiding Thinking Errors

The Learning Skills

After learning about the Psychological Keys to Student Success, you will learn some powerful learning strategies that psychologists and educators have known for years but that too few students know. I am going to give you insider information from the world of educational psychology that will help you learn more efficiently and at a deeper level. Remember, you don't want to just study. You want to learn! You can study information about traffic, road signs, and how a car works and then pass a written test about that stuff. But that does **not** make you a good driver. You have to practice, pay careful attention, test yourself, and value the importance of what you are learning and why in order to be a good driver.

The Psychological Skills

With over twenty years' experience in psychology, I believe there are some fundamental principles that will serve you well, in school and in life. Developing your capacity for self-awareness and using a handful of core concepts in psychology can make the thinking and learning skills in this book even more effective.

How You Will Achieve the Learning Objectives

By learning and practicing the thinking, learning, and psychological skills in this book, you will also develop important personal characteristics. That is the "how" part in the learning objectives. Let me highlight some of the characteristics for you.

First, let's consider something called *perceived academic control* (PAC). This is how much you believe you can influence and predict your own academic success. In high school, a lot of work was done for you by the teacher (e.g., scheduling, monitoring attendance, recognizing you needed help). In college, you must do these things for yourself. Developing perceived academic control will allow you to:

- meet the increased demands of college courses, engage more during classes, monitor and increase effort, increase critical thinking, use more effective studying methods, and obtain a better grades[4,5,6]

- experience more enjoyment, pride, and hope and less boredom, anxiety, and anger[7,8]
- persist and get higher grades[9]
- improve your psychological well-being.[10]

As I said at the beginning of this chapter, even the best schools and teachers cannot guarantee your success. Guess what -- research shows that good teaching helps students higher in perceived academic control more than those lower in perceived academic control.[11] That is why it is so important for you to develop PAC. Think about it this way: it is easier for someone who can run ten miles to run an additional two miles than it is for someone who can only run one mile to suddenly run three. In both cases, you're adding two miles of distance but the person with better training and endurance will do that more easily than someone with less training and endurance.

A second important personal characteristic is **resilience**, the ability to bounce back after setbacks. Research has shown it predicts academic achievement. Resilient people have:

- positive coping strategies that are flexible and adaptive
- a sense of control over their lives (psychologists would call this an internal "locus of control")
- a willingness to ask for help
- self-confidence
- impulse control
- good communication and people skills
- greater social maturity
- sense of responsibility
- desire to accomplish tasks.[12]

As you read this book and develop more effective thinking, learning, and psychology skills, you will be developing resilience at the same time.

Third, while personal control and resilience are particularly important characteristics for students, there are many others that will help you in school and throughout your life. Having a positive attitude, internal motivation, passion for your long-term goals, and maintaining effort despite setbacks are examples of personal characteristics associated with success.[13,14,15,16]

Students with a sense of responsibility, resourcefulness, determination, good time management skills, and who value education are more likely to successfully finish school.[17,18] The more you practice the many skills in this book, the more you will be establishing positive habits that will help you succeed in the classroom and beyond!

Fourth is something called **productive persistence**. The Carnegie Foundation for the Advancement of Teaching defines this as tenacity and the use of good strategies.[19] Tenacity means you keep up with your studying and attendance even when the going gets tough. Work all day? You still study for an exam even though you are tired. Class not going well? You talk to your instructor, study harder, and refuse to give up. That's tenacity.

When you're dealing with hard classes, information you don't understand, deadlines, low grades, negative feedback, bad teachers -- not to mention all the stuff in your life outside of school -- studying skills won't help you. When life is tough, you don't make flashcards and memorize definitions. But these personal characteristics will help deal with difficult circumstances, inside and outside of school.

So, Let's Begin

The findings I am sharing in this book are based on research, not opinions. The tiny numbers you see after many sentences refer to actual research done by scientific experts in the psychology and education fields. I've pulled together hundreds of these scientific discoveries (all listed in the Notes section at the end of the book) and translated them into plain English so you can know what scientists know about what works -- and what doesn't work -- when it comes to learning and succeeding in college. Ordinary "studying" books do not give you that.

Many students would not choose to read a book about how to learn, especially if it isn't required. But you did. That tells me you are already on your way to being a more reflective and effective student.

I am excited thinking about what we are going to accomplish together. Are you ready? Let's go!

SECTION 2:
THINKING SKILLS

MOTIVATION – THE BEGINNING

Learning how to think will help you spend more time pursuing your goals and less time avoiding your fears.

In psychology, motivation can be considered from many points of view. Sometimes motivation comes from *instincts*. These are genetically based, pre-programmed behaviors that help us survive. Running away from danger and flinching when you are surprised by a loud noise are instincts. Other times motivation is based on *needs*. These are requirements you must fulfill. Eating and sleeping are examples of needs.

There is an obvious relationship between instincts and needs when it comes to survival. For example, we have a need to eat. If we do not meet this need, we will die. Our instinct, therefore, is to find and consume food. An animal's instinct might be to kill another animal for food, whereas our instinct, as it has evolved over time, is to simply walk to the refrigerator and snarf down whatever we want. Instincts and needs motivate basic behaviors.

Abraham Maslow is a famous psychologist who suggested that motivation is guided by a hierarchy of needs, where basic needs like hunger must be met before higher-order needs such as getting an education. Feel free to Google "Maslow's Hierarchy of Needs" if you are curious and want more details.

Another point of view about motivation comes from the behavioral perspective in psychology. Most famously, B. F. Skinner promoted the view that we learn to do (and not do) certain behaviors based on the rewards (and punishments) we receive. Building on the ideas of E. L. Thorndike, Skinner demonstrated that rewards increase the chance you will perform a behavior again, while punishment decreases the chance you will do a behavior again. You understand this already because your parents used rewards and punishments to teach you what to do and what not to do. Rewards and punishments can be strong motivators.

When it comes to academic motivation, psychologist Henry Murray suggested that you have a "need to achieve." He believed that people have a natural desire "to overcome obstacles, to exercise power, [and] to strive to do something difficult as well as, and as quickly as, possible."[1]

Research by David McClelland and John Atkinson expanded on Murray's idea. McClelland explained that we "approach," or pursue, what we want because of a strong need for achievement. Can you think of a goal you set for yourself because you really wanted to achieve something?

Atkinson agreed with McClelland but added we have an equally important and opposite "need to avoid failure."[2,3] That need leads us to move away from, or avoid, what we do not want. Can you think of something you tried to make sure *did not* happen, such as looking "stupid" or getting in trouble?

Unfortunately, the motivation to avoid failure can sometimes hurt you.[4] For example, trying to avoid failure can prevent you from pursuing your goals and decrease your self-esteem, sense of personal control, and life satisfaction. The motivation to avoid failure also reduces self-regulation, college persistence, and grade point average.[5] Students who are strongly motivated to protect themselves against failure are also least likely to take responsibility for their failures and are more likely to blame others when something goes wrong.[6,7] All that stuff should sound bad, because it is. Fear is a strong motivator, but in school, it can get in your way.

Another interesting perspective about achievement motivation is the theory of planned behavior.[8] From this perspective, achievement is affected by how hard you are willing to try (i.e., your intentions), your ability to actually perform a behavior (called volitional control), and the situation. Situations and events come up in life that will change your intentions, your motivation, and your ability to do something. Anyone who decided to have children knows this!

The theory of planned behavior also explains how social pressure impacts your intentions and motivation. Here is an example: I have worked with many students who intend to study when they get home from school or work. However, the situation at home is busy because they have family responsibilities. Even though they sincerely want to study, they aren't always able to because caring for family is the priority.

Psychology often distinguishes between two types of motivation – intrinsic and extrinsic.

Intrinsic motivation is your desire to do something simply for its own sake. Intrinsic motivation comes from within you. Basically, you do something because you want to and you enjoy it. An example from my life was learning to fly. I got my private pilot's license simply because I wanted to. I love aviation.

Extrinsic motivation is your desire to gain a reward (or avoid a punishment) for doing something. Extrinsic motivation comes from outside you. It is often described as "a means to an end." An example of this might be going to work to get a paycheck (money is an external reward). You probably wouldn't go to work if you didn't get paid.

Both types of motivation impact your desire to approach good outcomes as suggested by David McClelland, and avoid bad outcomes as suggested by John Atkinson. You read, study, and complete assignments because you have an expectation about getting what you want and you then control your behavior as you pursue that goal.[9] As an example, if you love feeling knowledgeable, intrinsic motivation will lead you to study hard. At the same time, extrinsic motivation to have a higher-paying job (approach) and get out of poverty (avoid) will also lead you to study hard.

Here's something about motivation that may surprise you: *Some aspects of the school environment might actually decrease your motivation.*[10] Consider these three examples:

a. Being rewarded for doing something you enjoy can reduce intrinsic motivation. For example, if drawing is very personal and fulfilling, being told over and over that your drawings are good might take away from the enjoyment of it (believe it or not).

b. Deadlines can reduce intrinsic motivation by increasing pressure and making what you like to do feel like something you must do. For example, being told to finish a drawing by 9 a.m. tomorrow can reduce motivation to work on it tonight.

c. Being evaluated can reduce intrinsic motivation. For example, if you enjoy drawing, being graded can take away from your enjoyment of creating a new drawing.

Yes, rewards, deadlines, and evaluations are all part of school. However, before you blame academia for stripping away your motivation by imposing deadlines and evaluations, let me tell you that your perception is very important in this case. If you *think* that rewards, deadlines, and evaluations are controlling your choices and decisions, you may feel less intrinsically motivated.[11,12]

You can't *make* your classes or your teachers better in terms of the rewards, deadlines, or evaluations given. Some classes and teachers suck (I'm sorry to say). However, do you want to feel controlled by that? Our focus here is on what *you* can do. You may not get to choose your assignments, but how and when you do them is up to you. You can't choose your exams, but you can choose how to study for them. You can't control how your courses are taught or the prof's personality. But, no matter what, you can choose what you focus on in terms of "This is ok," versus "This sucks." Simple changes in **how you think** can help you control your motivation.

This book will show you **how to think** so that you don't suffer a loss of motivation due to circumstances like boring teachers and bad evaluations. Motivation includes setting a goal and then staying on task as you pursue that goal. It is the "thoughts, actions, or behaviors [you use] to influence [your] choice, effort, or persistence for academic tasks."[13] Motivation is about your willingness to keep working on something, especially when you get bored or distracted.

You are about to read the updated Psychological Keys to Student Success. Each Key addresses motivation in some way. In fact, the first six Psychological Keys directly influence motivation. There are even specific interventions to help students with their beliefs, attributions, goals and interest, self-efficacy, and self-regulated learning (Keys 1, 2, 3, 4, and 6). If you want to read a 39-page meta-analytic research study[14] about it, check the Notes for this chapter...or you can just take my word for it.

Are you ready? Are you motivated? I am! Follow me as we explore the ways *you* will become a better student.

KEY #1 - BELIEFS AND MINDSET

Your beliefs affect every class you take, every book you read, every moment you study, and every exam you complete.

"At its core, student success is determined by the attitudes and behaviors of individual students."[1] Did you catch that? Did ya? Developing a positive perception of yourself as a learner, and of the learning environment, is an important factor in deep learning.[2] Therefore, understanding the beliefs you have about yourself as a student and about school can help you understand how you perform in high school and college. Good teachers help students consider their personal strengths and weaknesses, think about them, and learn from those experiences.[3] I am trying to help you do exactly that. And please notice that says nothing about studying skills.

Imagine that a friend says to you, "It doesn't matter what I do. This stuff is too hard. I'm just stupid." How will these beliefs about the material and his intelligence affect his approach to studying? Those thoughts are not very motivating, are they?

Imagine that you run into another friend who says, "People ask too many questions in class. The instructor gave us the information. That's it. I hate it when people complicate things with stupid questions." If she believes that everything is black and white and that different viewpoints are useless, how will it affect her studying? What do you think – can you learn from the ideas, questions, and experiences of others?

It amazes me what many teachers and schools fail to teach. Many teachers don't come right out and tell you to consider your beliefs about education, knowledge, and learning. They frequently have you discuss your beliefs about "hot" topics such as religion, culture, public policy, discrimination, and sexual orientation. However, very few stress the importance of your personal beliefs about knowledge and learning. Really, how do people learn? How do *you* learn? What is knowledge, and what do you believe it means to be knowledgeable? Let's delve into this and explore the importance of your beliefs about education, knowledge, and learning.

Epistemological Beliefs

Epistemological beliefs are your ideas about knowledge and learning. "Epistemological" can be a tricky word to pronounce (try this: Ah-pist-em-ah-logical). These beliefs begin to develop when we are children. Young children have simple beliefs about knowledge and learning. Kids think that knowledge is absolute; it is about knowing "facts" and adults are experts who give them the facts. As we get older, our epistemological beliefs usually become more sophisticated; we realize that knowledge is complex and that learning develops slowly over time.

Educational psychologist Marlene Schommer identified four aspects of epistemological beliefs: innate ability, quick learning, simple knowledge, and certain knowledge.[4] Each aspect is like a dimension that ranges from naïve (i.e., simple) to sophisticated. The chart below summarizes information from an article Schommer wrote in 2005.[5] It also demonstrates my superior computer skills.

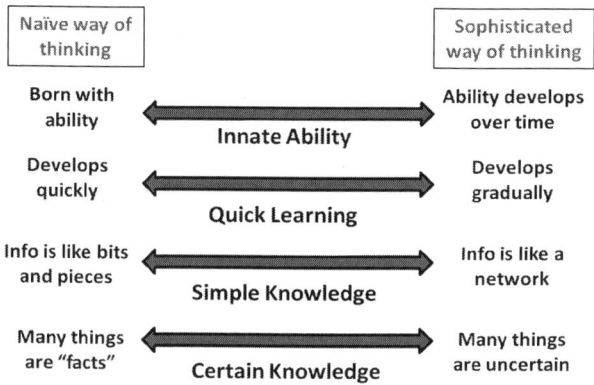

Here is an example from my own discipline. In psychology, we study human thoughts and emotions, which are complicated because they are affected by many factors and situations. There are no equations for our thoughts and emotions. For that reason, psychology can be difficult to learn if you *believe* that knowledge is simple and factual. Courses in psychology, philosophy, and ethics are complex, and often lack straightforward answers and facts.

Epistemological beliefs affect your approach to every class you take, every book you read, every moment you study, and every exam you complete. Understanding your beliefs about knowledge and learning will help explain your approach to different classes, and it will give you insight into your approach to school in general.

How Epistemological Beliefs Affect You – Some Research

Schommer's research demonstrated that students who believe that learning is quick and absolute were more likely to draw overly simplistic conclusions when reading and tended to perform more poorly on tests.[6] Conversely, students who believe that learning is gradual had higher GPAs.[7] Schommer's research also found that students who believe ability can improve over time valued education more and were more likely to persist in the face of academic challenges.[8]

Students who believe learning ability is something they are born with (or without) used fewer strategies "to connect their prior knowledge with new knowledge that is to be learned" and they did not "think critically about the information that they [were] processing."[9] Believing that ability is something you're born with can limit your learning. Students who have more sophisticated epistemological beliefs (i.e., the right side of the chart) show more effort, persistence, and critical thinking.[10,11]

Beyond Schommer's Work

I am going to extend your consideration of epistemological beliefs beyond those mentioned thus far. Let's look at other common beliefs students have. For each, decide what you believe and then think about whether the belief helps you or hurts you.

Your Learning History

Everyone has both positive and negative learning experiences in school. Those experiences, combined with your current educational goals, contribute to your beliefs and expectations about school and your academic abilities. Why do beliefs about your abilities matter? Here is an example. A study of 253 university students in a macroeconomics course showed that those who had a lower GPA were more likely to overestimate their exam performance. However, having a higher GPA, higher ACT scores, and previous experience with the topic all reduced the tendency to overestimate ability.[12] This means that having accurate beliefs about your ability is related to academic performance. Are your beliefs about your academic abilities accurate? We will consider this again in Keys #4 and #7.

"Easy" Classes

I'm sure you have signed up for a class and thought, "This will be easy." Many students, try to manage their schedules by selecting classes they hope will be less challenging to offset the workload of their required classes, which they often believe will be harder. For example, some students who have never taken a psychology class before believe that psychology is "all common sense." Believing it is easy, they don't study as much for psychology. The result is they get a bad grade on the first exam and spend the rest of the semester trying to recover. They learn the hard way that their belief was very inaccurate. Your beliefs about classes influence how seriously you take them.

What Classes "Should" Be Like

If you believe that a class or instructor does not fit with your goals or your preferred learning style, you might experience negative emotions such as boredom or anxiety. These feelings can distract you and lead to lower performance.[13] A common example occurs when a student thinks that college classes should have a lot of discussions and group work. When that student enrolls in an introductory course that is lecture-based, he may start to think about how the class is "pointless" and "boring" and how the teacher sucks. Those beliefs are big internal distractions, and they are entirely unnecessary. Rather than dwell on what you believe "should be," focus on the reality and deal with it.

What Teachers Should Be Like

What should and shouldn't teachers do? Your beliefs about this will affect your willingness to learn. Should teachers simply give out facts or should they challenge your beliefs, too? What if a teacher suggests something that is contrary to your religious or personal beliefs? Is that a sticking point you want to argue about or are you prepared to consider different perspectives as part of the educational process? Questions like these help you examine your epistemological beliefs.

A teacher can work hard using many different teaching strategies to make a class interesting. However, your perception of that teacher, the teaching strategies, and topics is what matters most. The teacher could be awesome (like me) but if you don't like him or if you don't care about the class, it doesn't matter what the teacher does. The most important factor is **how you think** about the teacher and the class. That's totally up to you.

How to Study for Exams

Another important belief is how to study for different types of exams. Many students adjust how they study based on the type of exam questions they expect to see and based on their belief about what the instructor expects of them on an exam.[14,15] Here is an example from my teaching experience: Students treat multiple choice exams like they are easy. They do not study as much, because they expect to recognize the correct answer in the answer choices. That is a faulty belief. Multiple choice questions can be tricky because the choices may be similar. Relying on recognition alone often leads students to feel like all the answer choices are correct. Don't you hate it when that happens? Well, guess what – you did it to yourself by not studying properly! I will teach you how to avoid this problem in the Powerful Learning Strategies section.

A 2009 research study asked 177 undergraduate students about their studying habits. Eighty-four percent reported simply re-reading material as a studying strategy, and 55 percent reported re-reading was their preferred strategy. A much more effective strategy is to practice recalling the information (i.e., close your book and try to remember what you read). Only 11 percent used this method, and only 1 percent said it was the preferred strategy. Another great studying strategy is to test yourself but only 18 percent of the students reported this strategy as part of their studying.[16] I will tell you a lot more about the power of self-testing later, too.

Here is one studying tip I give students: Imagine that you arrive late for an exam. Everyone is gone and you catch me as I'm leaving the class. You apologize and ask if you can still take the exam. I tell you to meet me in my office in 10 minutes. When you arrive I say, "Are you ready? I am going to ask you questions. Just tell me the answers." Right then, you will probably have an OMG moment. I'm not giving you the multiple choice exam. I'm giving you an oral exam.

In that scenario, if you would have known the exam was oral and not multiple choice, you probably would have studied differently (or more...or both). That simple realization reflects that you have different beliefs about different kinds of exams, and those beliefs guide how you study. I suggest that you study for all exams like you will have to explain everything to the professor. You will study much, much harder.

Time

Are you busy? Do you ever feel like there are not enough hours in the day? Do you believe that studying for easy classes should take less time than studying for harder classes? Do your expectations for how much time you have available to study match your professors' expectations about how much time is required to do well?

Please consider this statement about time: "According to both first-generation and traditional students, their time commitments inevitably reflected the amount of time that they had available, rather than the amount of time it would take to master the course material."[17] The question is, are you fitting college into your existing schedule or are you making college the main priority in your schedule?

As a college prof, I respect whatever you decide about your time and availability. However, your other commitments and decisions about time do not change the expectations and requirements in college courses. The time you have and the effort you give will be compared to the standards in the courses. Profs don't lower the standards to accommodate your schedule.

Your Belief About the Value of Education

Your motivation to achieve is influenced by how much you value education. This is important to your overall view of education, and in every class you take. In 2004, three researchers explained that your sense of the value of classes has four parts: how important you think the class is, how interesting you find the material, how useful you think the material is, and any costs or problems associated with taking the class.[18] This means that *how you think* about the value of classes influences your motivation in those classes.

Wrapping Up Epistemological Beliefs

Whatever your beliefs are, the ones that stand out to you are most likely to influence how you approach school. In the words of Icek Ajzen, "these salient beliefs...are considered to be the prevailing determinants of a person's intentions and actions."[19] That is an eloquent way of saying that your beliefs are one of the main factors that influence what you do in school.

Mindset – A Type of Belief

Psychologist Carol Dweck researches and teaches about "implicit theories of intelligence." These are your beliefs about how changeable intelligence is. Students who believe intelligence can be developed and increased have an "incremental theory of intelligence." This is called a "growth mindset." Alternatively, students who believe intelligence is unchangeable have an "entity theory of intelligence." This is called a "fixed mindset." There appears to be an even split between people who hold growth mindsets and those who hold fixed mindsets (40 percent growth mindset; 40 percent fixed mindset; 20 percent undecided).[20]

What do you believe? Is intelligence something you can improve (growth mindset) or do you believe intelligence is something you're just born with (fixed mindset)? Research has shown there are advantages associated with having a growth mindset. Students who have a growth mindset:

a. focus on the importance of learning for understanding, not just getting high grades;

b. see that making more effort is a sign of getting smarter, *not* a sign that something is too hard or that they are not smart enough;

c. feel that having trouble during a task is a sign of needing to work harder, not a lack of ability;

d. describe their performance (you will see this in Key #2) in terms of their effort and use of strategies rather than their intelligence;

e. hold a mastery achievement goal orientation (you will see this in Key #3);

f. experience enjoyment from learning, even when they are not naturally "good at" a topic;

g. are more likely to develop confidence (you will see this in Key #4) as they learn, even if learning is a struggle;

h. feel less anxiety; and

i. retry things they struggled with (alternatively, students with a fixed mindset tend to avoid things they didn't do well on and are less likely to learn from mistakes).[21]

You can think about the growth and fixed mindsets in terms of your overall intelligence, but you can also think of mindsets in terms of specific abilities too. For example, are you good at math or do you suck at it? If you think you suck at math (fixed mindset) and are struggling with a math problem, you are more likely to give up. If you think math is a skill you can improve (growth mindset) and you run into a tough math problem, you are more likely to keep trying.

One consistent finding in the research is that a person's mindset varies from ability to ability. For example, you can have a growth mindset about your writing ability but a fixed mindset about your drawing ability: "If I practice writing, I know I'll get better at it. But, I don't think I'll ever be good at drawing." It is pretty easy to see how your beliefs about your own abilities and intelligence will affect your attitude toward classes.

How to Develop a Growth Mindset

Developing beliefs that energize and motivate you is a process and it takes a little practice, especially at times when you feel a frustrated or unsure of yourself. Accepting yourself as you are right now and understanding others have similar struggles and challenges is important. With that realization, you can start to grow by learning new things and tackling new and exciting challenges.

Here are some ideas about developing a growth mindset.[22,23,24,25]

- Google "You Can Grow Your Intelligence" and read the brief article at Mindset Works.

- The brain is literally able to grow and rewire its connections when we learn new things. So, you can learn even the most difficult things with practice.

- Believing you can improve leads your brain to be more active.

- Think about mistakes as opportunities to learn, not as failures.

- Understand that you can always improve.

- When struggling, do not struggle alone. Ask for help.

- Do not wait for feedback from teachers. Go ask for it.

- When you're having trouble with something, it is simply something you haven't gotten *yet*.

- Learn new and different studying techniques. The more studying tools you have, the more flexible your learning is.

- Focus on your effort, not just grades.

- Set small, well-defined, measurable goals for your school work *every day*.

One of the most important pieces of advice I give all my students is to **treat everything in school like it is a skill**. Reading is a skill. Writing papers is a skill. Math is a skill. Studying is a skill. Taking exams is a skill. Skills are something you can practice and develop, so there is no reason you cannot get really good at everything in school. Thinking this way is the growth mindset!

FINAL THOUGHTS

Becoming aware of your beliefs about knowledge, learning, intelligence, and specific school-related abilities can help you harness the power of helpful beliefs and work to change the unhelpful beliefs. Beliefs are like a filter through which all your experiences pass. If the beliefs are bad, your experience will be bad. If the beliefs are good . . . I'll let you finish that sentence.

One last point: Teachers often go on and on about "critical thinking." Part of critical thinking requires you to examine your beliefs. The right-hand column (sophisticated ways of thinking) in the chart shown earlier in this chapter reflects some of the main ideas associated with critical thinking. One researcher explained that "students should have the capacity and the inclination to question their intuitive beliefs, identify misconceptions, and replace them with a new explanatory framework."[26] That is what I'm trying to help you do - question your beliefs about learning and develop beliefs that will serve you better. I am trying to help you develop "college knowledge,"[27] a better set of beliefs about what it means to prepare for, be in, and successfully complete school.

Now that you are considering your beliefs and how they impact your school performance, it is time to think about how you explain your performance. Why do you get good (or bad) grades on assignments, quizzes, and exams? It is time for Psychological Key #2 – Attributions.

KEY #2 – ATTRIBUTIONS

How you explain what happens to you affects your mood, motivation, school success, and even your relationships.

We constantly try to figure out why people do what they do and why things happen the way they do. Why did you yell at your friend? Why did you smile at that stranger? Why did that driver cut you off? Why did Mother Theresa help people? WHY? WHY? WHY?

Related to school, why might you get an A on an exam? Now think of why you might get a failing grade. There are reasons that explain the results you get, right?

An attribution is your attempt to explain why a behavior or event happened. Any time you do something or something happens around you, you will try to explain why you did it or why it happened. How you make attributions reflects your beliefs, influences your motivation, and affects your emotions. It impacts everything about your school experience from your attendance to your studying habits to your grades. As we did with Key #1 (Beliefs & Mindset), we are focusing on **how you think**.

According to Bernard Weiner, attributions are a "search for understanding" and a "spring for action."[1] To explain your academic successes and failures, you evaluate your ability, effort, the difficulty of the task, and things like luck and circumstances.[2] Do you think about your ability and effort when you get a grade on an assignment? Do you consider how hard an exam was when you try to explain your grade? Do you consider luck or other circumstances?

Weiner suggested and studied three aspects of attributions: locus, stability, and control.[3] Let's look at each.

The **locus** aspect of an attribution can be internal or external. When you make an **internal** attribution, you are saying the cause of the behavior or event is due to a characteristic of a person. When you make an **external** attribution, you are saying the cause of the behavior or event comes from the situation, not the person.

The **stability** aspect of an attribution can be stable or unstable. When you make a **stable** attribution, you are saying the cause of the behavior or event will probably be the same regardless of the situation. When you make an **unstable** attribution, you are saying the cause of the behavior or event will probably change depending on the situation.

The **control** aspect of an attribution can be controllable or uncontrollable. When you make a **controllable** attribution, you are saying the cause of the behavior or event is something the person can influence. When you make an **uncontrollable** attribution, you are saying the cause of the behavior or event is something the person cannot influence.

At the beginning of this chapter I asked you reasons why you might get a good grade on an exam. I also asked you to explain why you might get a bad grade. Let's look at the example of you trying to explain why you might get a bad grade. Let's pretend you attribute poor performance to "being stupid." Looking at the three aspects of attributions outlined by Weiner, being "stupid" is internal, stable, and uncontrollable. "Stupidity" is a personal quality (internal), it is unlikely to change quickly (stable), and a lot of people believe it isn't something you can do a lot about (it is uncontrollable *if* you believe that intelligence is something you're born with or without).

As you can see, beliefs (Key #1) and attributions are connected. If you believe intelligence is unchangeable, that means you have a fixed mindset. In that case, you are more likely to attribute success to being smart and failure to being stupid. Either way, the attribution is internal, stable, and uncontrollable. If you are on the smart end of this judgment, you will feel successful and be motivated to do well again in the future. However, in our example of doing poorly and attributing it to "stupidity," your feelings will be unpleasant and your motivation will be reduced.

If you develop a growth mindset and do poorly on an exam, your belief is that intelligence is unstable (that it can change). In this case, you may still attribute your grade to "stupidity" but you will be motivated to work harder because you believe you can become smarter. The attribution is still internal but now it is changeable and controllable based on your belief that you can get smarter.

The third aspect of attributions, control, highlights the connection between behavior and outcomes as well as how much you believe you are capable of doing the necessary behavior.[4] Do you remember the first learning objective about perceived academic control? Well, check this out. A study of 524 college students found that students higher in perceived academic control tried harder, reported higher motivation, used more self-monitoring strategies, experienced less boredom and anxiety, and got higher grades.[5] In other words, if you think grades are something you can control, you will do better. Research has also shown that students who are low in perceived academic control are less likely to benefit from quality teaching.[6] If you tend to blame academic problems on everything and everyone else, it won't matter how good the teacher is. You won't benefit from good teaching unless you take responsibility for your learning and the results you get.

Accepting responsibility for poor performance can be a little tricky in terms of attributions. As you already saw, saying you are stupid is a form of "owning" poor performance but that is unmotivating if you have a fixed mindset. However, saying that you didn't try hard enough or that you didn't practice enough is something you can control. Lack of effort or practice is clearly changeable. That can motivate you. *It is important to make internal attributions that are controllable.*

When you do poorly, it is much better to attribute that result to internal but controllable and unstable (changeable) factors such as effort, because it allows you to still feel good about yourself and know you can avoid a similar problem in the future by changing your behavior.[7] In other words, attributing poor performance to something you can control, such as making more effort or paying closer attention, means that you can reduce the chance of poor performance in the future. You can improve. That also fits perfectly with a growth mindset.

Some attributions can be inspiring while others can be very unmotivating. It is better to make internal attributions for success AND failure. Internal attributions put you "in the driver's seat." If you do well, take credit for it. If you do poorly, own it. This is what Julian Rotter (1966) called "locus of control," and it is the first aspect of attributions.[8] Here is the important question: Is what happens to you in school up to you, or is up to things outside you?

Taking credit for your success is internal and motivating. However, some students make external attributions for their successes. That's right. They don't take credit for their success. Sometimes this is totally okay. Sometimes it is not. If you get a lot of help and attribute your success to that help, it may just be a sign of gratitude and a recognition that you did well, in part, because of the help you got. That's great and is much more common in other cultures.

Alternatively, if you do well and say, "The instructor just made an easy exam" or "I got lucky," these external attributions for success might reduce motivation by making it feel like you had nothing to do with your own success.

When Are You Most Motivated to Understand "Why?"

There are situations when you are strongly motivated to explain why a behavior or event occurred. For example, you are more likely to want to explain bad and/or unexpected results. Doing poorly does not have to mean that you get an F; it can be that you achieve at a level that is lower than what you expected or wanted.[9]

Another time you are motivated to explain your results is when events are unexpected (good or bad), especially if the outcome or event is personally relevant. For example, when you are surprised by a grade that is lower than expected, that outcome is experienced as poor, unexpected, and very personally relevant to your course grade. In that case, you will be very motivated to explain *why*. With your new understanding of attributions, what will happen if you attribute the lower-than-expected grade to stupidity? How about lack of effort? How would these two different attributions affect your feelings and subsequent motivation and behavior? Remember, saying you are stupid is usually unmotivating. Also, remember that attributing a poor grade to lack of effort may upset you but the amount of effort you make is something you can change.

I just told you that people are more likely to try and explain poor results. I believe you should also intentionally think about your good results. How can you repeat success if you don't understand what you did to achieve it? Always think about what you did to achieve success so that you can repeat it. At the same time, you should consider situational factors so you can understand that what you did in one situation/class might not always work in a different situation/class. Pay attention to *both* personal and situational factors.

Expectations and Your Attributions

Your expectations (beliefs) influence how you explain your academic results. Research suggests that your expectations come from your ideas about your own ability and how much effort you plan to make,[10] how much your achievement efforts have been reinforced,[11] and social aspects of the school environment such as competition and the feedback you receive.[12]

Expectations are a type of belief (Key #1) and are connected to your attributions. In a general sense, students who do well in high school enter college expecting to continue getting good grades. That belief has with it the attributional characteristic of stability: "I do well in school." If this describes your thinking, how will you respond in college if you get a lower grade than you wanted? If you say, "College is hard and I can't do it because all classes will be like this," that attribution will reduce your motivation. If you say, "I am smart because I did well in high school, but I obviously need to work harder in college," that internal attribution suggests you can do something about the situation (it is changeable and controllable). That is much better for your motivation and reflects a growth mindset.

Emotions and Your Attributions

Our emotions are related to the results we get. There are basic emotions that are *"outcome-dependent"* and there are emotions that are *"attribution-dependent."*[13,14] Outcome-dependent emotions are the feelings you get right when something happens. Attribution-dependent emotions are the feelings you get after you think about why something happened.

Here is an example. When you get a paper back with a big A+ at the top, you will feel happy. That is the simple, outcome-dependent emotion. After that, when you think about how hard you worked on the paper, you might feel proud and satisfied. Those are the attribution-dependent emotions. However, if you attribute your good grade to luck, the attribution-dependent emotion might be relief instead of pride. These emotions can influence your motivation and behavior differently.

Now imagine that you get your paper back and it has a big, red D at the top. You might feel angry or worried. Those are outcome-dependent emotions. Then you have to think about why you got a D and make an attribution. If you attribute getting a D to stupidity, you may feel hopeless and sad. In that case, you may be motivated to avoid academic tasks (this can contribute a lot to procrastination, especially for those who fear failure). If, however, you attribute the D to an internal, unstable, and controllable factor like a lack of effort, you may feel disappointed in yourself and, therefore, be motivated to do better next time. Once again, **how you do** hinges on **how you think**.

Attribution Errors

The confidence you have in your academic skills is important, but it must also be accurate. Thinking you are a better student than you are can create significant attributional errors, such as blaming low grades on a teacher. Similarly, thinking you are a weak student when you are capable can lead to errors too, such as thinking you are stupid when you are not (more common for students who fear failure and have a fixed mindset).

When it comes to your beliefs and attributions, I want you to develop greater self-awareness and the ability to assess yourself accurately. Attributions are only helpful and great sources of learning and motivation to the extent they are realistic and accurate. For example, attributions of success will not be believable if you keep failing, and attributions of low effort for failure will be meaningless if you try really hard but still fail.[15]

In order to make accurate attributions about a behavior or event, you need to consider both personal characteristics and aspects of the situation. Consider the following two scenarios:

a. *You* consistently arrive late to class and the teacher finally tells you that your behavior is disruptive and unacceptable.

b. *A classmate* you don't know consistently arrives late to class and the teacher finally tells the student that his behavior is disruptive and unacceptable.

So, to what do you attribute your own consistent tardiness and to what do you attribute your classmate being consistently tardy? Research shows you are more likely to attribute your own tardiness to situational factors such as bad traffic or having back-to-back classes (external attribution). However, you are more likely to attribute the same bad behavior of your classmate to his/her personal characteristics such as being disrespectful or inconsiderate (internal attribution).

There are three attributional biases that are common in Western psychology (people in other cultures make attributions differently so this doesn't apply equally to everyone). The first is called the ***self-serving bias***. It says we are more likely to attribute our own success to personal qualities but attribute our own bad behavior to situational factors. For example, when you get an A on a test you are more likely to say you are a great student, but when you get a D you are more likely to say that the test was too hard.

The second bias, called the ***fundamental attribution error***, occurs when we judge the behavior of others. We are more likely to attribute other people's bad behavior or results to their personal qualities and are less likely to consider the situation. For example, when a classmate fails an exam, you are more likely to say that the she is "dumb" instead of considering that she has two jobs and doesn't have as much time to study as she wants.

The third bias is called the ***actor-observer bias***. When you are actively part of a situation, you make different attributions about behavior than if you are an observer of the situation. For example, when you give a presentation (i.e., you are the "actor") and you feel nervous, you might attribute your nervousness to the instructor looking at you and writing stuff down. That is, you make an external attribution for your nervousness; you feel that way because of what is happening outside of you. However, when someone else is doing a presentation (i.e., now you are an "observer") and looks nervous, you are more likely to attribute her nervousness to things like lack of preparation or shyness. You make an internal attribution for her nervousness. You say she is nervous because of something about her. It is the same situation, but your attribution changes depending on whether you are in the situation or if you are watching the situation.

Training Yourself to Make Better Attributions

There is a lot of research showing the benefits of making internal, controllable, and unstable (changeable) attributions.[16,17,18,19,20,21]

There are specific interventions designed to help students learn how to make these more effective attributions.

This Psychological Key to Student Success has shown you the difference between helpful and unhelpful attributions. By intentionally making internal, controllable, and unstable attributions, you can have the following benefits:[22,23,24,25]

- stronger pursuit of your goals

- increased motivation and persistence

- increased effort

- increased perceived academic control

- more effective approach to challenges and failures

- development of a growth mindset

- creation of mastery goals (the next Psychological Key)

- more realistic expectations for performance

- strengthened feelings of personal responsibility

- improved grades

- reduced fear of failure

- decreased hopelessness, worthlessness, and anxiety

- decreased likelihood of dropping classes.

FINAL THOUGHTS

I hope this Key has you considering how you explain your behavior and the results you get. You should also be thinking about how you explain the behavior of your teachers and classmates. Attributions strongly influence your motivation, feelings, and approach to school.

I have a bias: I think this Key is very important. Attributions affect your self-esteem, relationships, moods, expectations, and even your mental health. As such, they have great power over your experience. You need to start recognizing how you make attributions and how that influences you in school...and in life.

When you think about your personal beliefs (Key #1) and the attributions (Key #2) you make, you can see the importance of **how you think**. You are building greater perceived academic control by examining your beliefs, mindset, and ways of making attributions and seeing how it all affects your motivation. You have already started improving your chances for success.

I really appreciate your effort so far! Next, we will consider your goals and how they can impact your success as a student.

KEY #3 – ACHIEVEMENT GOALS & INTEREST

Goals help you focus on the future. They are a powerful source of motivation and represent your beliefs, hopes, and dreams.

If I asked you what an achievement goal is, you might say, "It is what a person wants to accomplish in school." Does that sound about right? Well, believe it or not, an achievement goal has become a tricky thing for psychologists to define. Leave it to psychology to take two terms that are easy to understand (achievement and goals), mash them together, and make a complicated term.

Because this concept is one of the Psychological Keys to Student Success, I'll help you navigate through the mess psychology has made. (Yes, I'm making fun of my own discipline!) Please bear with me as I tell you what psychology says about this concept. You are about to read some complicated definitions. However, as is my goal in this book, I will help you break them down into something useful.

Goals

Goals "represent students' perceptions and beliefs about the purposes of academic achievement."[1] They help you identify what you want to achieve, how to evaluate your own efforts toward the goal, and what you need to do to stay on track (like increasing motivation and avoiding distractions).[2,3] Basically, goals allow you to define what you want, how to get it, and how to evaluate your efforts.

Achievement Goals

In psychology, there is a specific definition of goals related to how you approach school. Achievement goals are not simply about getting good grades; they are about how you define competence.[4] They are about your motivation to become skilled at something. Psychologist Carol Ames defined an achievement goal as "an integrated pattern of beliefs, attributions, and affect that produces the intentions of behavior and that is represented by different ways of approaching, engaging in, and responding to achievement type activities."[5]

I don't blame you if you are thinking, "OMG. What does that mean?" Well, hang on. Let's pick the definition apart and you will see it is useful. Notice that the first two things she mentioned are the first two Psychological Keys to Student Success – beliefs and attributions. Basically, the quotation says that what you think (i.e., your beliefs) and how you explain things (i.e., your attributions) influence whether you enroll in school, go to classes, study for exams, and learn from feedback. See, that wasn't so bad.

Are you ready to really shake your head? Here's another definition: an achievement goal is a "future-focused cognitive representation that guides behavior to a competence-related end state that the individual is committed to either approach or avoid."[6]

WHAT? LOL. Psychologists are funny. They don't always put things in terms that people can understand (and I think they need to go outside and play more often). Well, let's pick that definition apart too and find something useful. In that quotation, achievement goals are given several qualities.

a. Goals help you focus on what you want to accomplish in the future. They give you a purpose. That sounds like a goal, right? OK, so far, so good.

b. Goals are something you think about and can "see" in your mind. They give you a vision in your mind about your future.

c. Goals lead you to try and develop skills. You gotta know how to do stuff, right?

d. Goals might actually lead you to avoid some things too. Don't get hung up on the "avoid" part. I promise to explain that later. Keep reading.

Here is one last definition. Paul Pintrich suggested that achievement goals are like a set of beliefs about success, effort, and our abilities.[7] Obviously, that means this third Psychological Key is related to the first (Beliefs & Mindset).

Let's look at different types of achievement goals and see how they affect your approach to classes, and school in general.

Types of Achievement Goal Orientations

There are two general types of achievement goals students have when they take a class. They are called mastery goals and performance goals. You have a *mastery goal orientation* when you want to gain new knowledge and develop skills. You have a *performance goal orientation* when you want to prove your ability compared to others. The distinction is that if mastery is your goal, you want to *be good* at something and *improve* your ability. But, with a performance goal, you want to *look like* you are good at something and *prove* your ability.

Another way of describing the difference between mastery and performance goals comes from the seminal work (that means it was very influential) of Carol Dweck and Ellen Leggett.[8] Look at this comparison:

Mastery focus	Performance focus
Want to improve ability	Concerned with proving ability
Compare progress to own skill and knowledge	Compare own knowledge and skill to that of others
Focus on learning	Focus on grades
Want to please themselves	Want to impress others
Failure is experienced as a learning opportunity	Failure is often experienced as a threat

Here is an example of how these goals can help you or hurt you. Pretend your present knowledge in psychology is pretty low. You are totally new to the subject. You work hard because you want to improve your knowledge. You study hard and after a few weeks you notice that your understanding has increased. Even though you haven't achieved the ultimate level of knowledge you are striving for, you are improving. That is motivating, so you keep pursuing more knowledge. You compare what you know now with what you knew before and focus on your own improvement. This reflects a growth mindset and a mastery goal.

Now consider performance goals. Your focus is on grades and how your grades compare to the grades others are getting. Right now, let's say your general knowledge in psychology is a 3/10. You notice that others are 7/10. This motivates you to beat their scores. You study hard and increase your grades so you are an 8/10.

In the example above, the performance goal served you well. Your grades got better. That's not a bad thing. Let me show you when a performance goal is a problem.

Consider again that your current knowledge level in psychology is a 3/10 but the people you are comparing yourself to are only a 4/10. You don't have to work very hard or know very much to beat them. So, when you get yourself up to a 5/10, you are the BEST. You don't know very much, but you are now better than everyone else. Once you are the "best" you won't be as motivated to continue learning. That is a down side to a performance goal.

Another potential problem with performance goals is that comparing yourself to others might make you worry about appearing unskilled or incompetent, especially if you compare yourself to people who are good at something. That can make you want to avoid challenging tasks and evaluations (remember, I said some goals might lead you to avoid things).

Mastery Goals Are Good

Students who are mastery-focused have some desirable characteristics. They want to learn for the sake of learning. They have intrinsic motivation. This often relates to having more interest in an area (or in learning, in general). They seek out and enjoy a challenge and will keep trying when things are difficult (that's persistence). They learn from the feedback they receive, even when the feedback is "negative."

Students who are mastery-oriented are more likely to have a growth mindset. They are likely to experience positive emotions associated with learning, be open to working together with other students, and be open to sharing and understanding opinions.[9] They tend to make internal and controllable attributions about successes and failures. They see effort as the path to learning and see any failures as a sign they used the wrong learning strategy, not as an indication of incompetence.[10]

Related to Key #4, which you will read about next, mastery students are more likely to "interpret feedback in terms of their progress, thereby supporting their self-efficacy."[11] That means feedback, good and bad, helps them feel more confident because it helps them learn and improve.

Heidi Grant and Carol Dweck conducted a series of studies and found several benefits associated with mastery goals. Mastery-oriented students:

    a. viewed "negative" feedback about their work as an opportunity to learn and improve. As you already learned, attributions (Key #2) are important. Thinking you can improve is more motivating than thinking you're stupid.

    b. had more interest and intrinsic motivation for learning.

    c. demonstrated better planning and more persistence toward their desired academic outcomes.[12]

Students with mastery goals have a more positive attitude toward learning and believe that effort will lead to success.[13,14] Mastery goals are related to more interest, effort, cooperation, help-seeking, self-regulated learning, and better learning strategies.[15,16] Research has also demonstrated that mastery goals increase positive emotions, including pride and hope, and buffer students against negative emotions, like boredom, anger, hopelessness, and shame.[17]

Performance Goals – Some Ups and Downs

Performance goals are not just one, straight-forward thing. Students with performance goals may experience different kinds of motivation. One type of motivation is to appear competent and intelligent. With an *appearance motivation*, you may not care about how others have done on an assignment or exam as long as you have impressed an audience (such as the teacher). The second type of motivation occurs when you are concerned with comparing your abilities to that of others. This is called *normative motivation*. You would compare your grade with how other students did.

Students with appearance motivation and students with normative motivation have one thing in common – they are both concerned about being evaluated.[18]

There are two types of performance goals. If you have a *performance-approach* goal, you will be concerned with looking competent but you will tackle challenges like they are opportunities. This increases concentration and intrinsic motivation. You will invest yourself in the activity.

Alternatively, a *performance-avoidance* goal will make you avoid looking incompetent or stupid. Challenges are seen as a threat. If something is difficult, you will try to protect yourself against failure and are more likely to make up phony excuses when you do badly. You are more likely to be distracted, procrastinate, and/or give up. Sadly, the desire to avoid failure can be a very powerful motivator – one with many negative consequences.[19]

Andrew Elliot and Judith Harackiewicz did some interesting research on the approach and avoidance distinction. First, they found that students with mastery, performance-approach, and performance-avoidance goals all showed effort and ability on a task. That's right. All the students tried hard and could do the task given by the researchers. However, students with the performance-avoidance goal were afraid to fail. This reduced their intrinsic motivation. They were less persistent when having trouble with a task and focused more on themselves instead of the task. That was like a big internal distraction and it left them unable to enjoy the task in the same way as those with a mastery or performance-approach goal.[20]

Here are some other interesting research findings. Fears and anxiety experienced by students with avoidance goals disrupt studying for exams, which negatively affects exam performance.[21] Students who begin a semester with performance-approach goals may actually shift to performance-avoidance goals if they do poorly on the first exam.[22] As well, students with performance-avoidance goals may have greater fear of failure and lower expectations about their own competence.[23] Students who fear failure actually end up focusing more on protecting their self-worth than striving to achieve.[24]

There is also research that shows students with avoidance goals select less challenging tasks in the first place. Students with performance-avoidance goals may experience more boredom, anger, anxiety, hopelessness, and shame and those negative emotions can lead to poorer academic achievement.[25,26]

One thing I notice in my classes when I talk about these different goals is the look on some students' faces. I can see that they worry because they recognize a performance-avoidance orientation in themselves. If you are one of those students reading this right now, please ***do not*** give up. Remember, with effort you can improve and change (you can develop a growth mindset). Keep reading. There is good news coming.

Achievement Goals – General or Specific?

You can have different achievement goals in different settings. For example, you might have a mastery orientation in chemistry simply because you have great interest in it. However, you might have a performance-avoidance orientation in your philosophy class because you consistently feel incompetent. As a result, you might participate fully in chemistry but skip philosophy class. You might study for many hours for a small chemistry quiz but procrastinate terribly for a big philosophy exam.

Can I Be a Combination of Orientations?

You can have mastery goals and performance goals at the same time, and even in the same class. Let me share a personal example. When I was getting my bachelor's degree, I was interested in my psychology classes and had a ton of intrinsic motivation to understand all the material. That is the mastery orientation. I was also competitive and wanted to "beat" everyone on assignments and exams. That is the performance-approach orientation. Together, those two goal orientations served me well. I received the Dean of Arts medal when I graduated with my bachelor's degree. That means the school thought I was the coolest geek there (well, not quite but…lol).

How Students Define "Success" and Goal Orientations

I found a 2013 report interesting and want to share it briefly with you. Don't jump to any conclusions because it is only one report based on interviews with only 66 students. When asked, most of the students defined college success in terms of getting good grades. Most did not mention things like a desire to learn or wanting to explore and research new ideas.[27] What strikes me most about this is that getting good grades reflects a performance-goal orientation. As you have learned, that motivation can be good, but it can also be bad.

What do you think would happen if you asked your friends what it means to be successful in college? Would their answers reflect more performance goals or mastery goals? What would your answers be?

SUGGESTION: There was a technique I used with clients when I was a counselor. I used something known as the "miracle question." Here it is: *Imagine that, while you sleep tonight, a miracle happens. In the morning, how will you know that the miracle happened? What will be different?*

I am bringing this to your attention so you can apply it to your education. In your school experience, what would the miracle be?

Of course, you understand that the miracle is you, right? What can you *do* to make this "miracle" happen? This is a nifty little way to help you identify important educational goals and begin planning how to achieve them.

Goal Orientations – Summary

Now that you understand these achievement goals better, which one sounds most like your overall approach to school? Do you fall more toward the mastery or performance orientation? If you think you fall more toward the performance-avoidance orientation, keep reading. Simply reading this book is helping you develop thinking skills that promote the mastery and performance-approach goals.

I researched many articles (cool geek) about achievement goal orientations. Some of the information is straightforward. Most of it is complex. The mastery orientation benefits are many, and they are clear. However, we live in a competitive world. In cases of competition, a performance-approach orientation can help too. It is also important to be aware of the fear of failure and likelihood of procrastination associated with the performance-avoidance orientation. It can be crippling, but it is something you can change by developing a growth mindset and teaching yourself to make internal, controllable attributions.

Interest

Interest is part of both mastery and performance goals and it is also a great source of motivation to learn. Research has shown that interest is associated with being more engaged in learning, increased attention, positive emotions, and getting higher grades.[28,29]

Interest can be like a personality characteristic. Some people are just naturally curious and interested in many things. When that is true, motivation is intrinsic. Interest also depends on the situation. When interest is situational, motivation comes from qualities of the topic/situation.

A quick example from my own experience might help. I was drawn to psychology because of my general interest in understanding and helping people. That interest is just part of who I am (individual, intrinsically motivated interest). In any given psychology class, however, my situational interests varied. For example, I found information about psychiatric hospitals fascinating in the moment, but I was never interested in working in one.

Another example from my personal life is about aviation. Ever since I was a kid, I have been interested in flight. I can't explain why. I just think it is really cool. In 2000, I earned a private pilot's license just because of my life-long interest. To get that license, however, I had to learn about some topics I wasn't naturally interested in, such as engines and physics. Because they were part of aviation though, learning about them became interesting.

There is a lot of research about how teachers can capture a student's interest.[30,31] The research shows that it is important for teachers to stimulate interest in students and to understand students' different learning styles. But I did not write a book about what teachers should do for you to be successful. I wrote a book for *you* about what *you* can do to be successful. Our consideration of interest, therefore, must focus on *your* role in your own level of interest in school. It is equally important for you to understand that teachers don't have any control over the interests you have (or don't have) when you enroll in their classes.[32]

Suggestions

Here are some ideas about how you can create, maintain, and pursue your interests. I hate the idea of you sitting back waiting for someone or something else to "make" you interested in a topic, assignment, or class. That doesn't fit in either the mastery or the performance goal orientations. It also doesn't fit with personal responsibility, perceived academic control, or helpful attributions.

SUGGESTION #1: Interest is a function of how much you "like" something, but it also relates to how useful and personally relevant you think it is. Teachers try to point out the usefulness of a topic, but they can't tell you exactly how to apply the topic to *your* experience. They give examples, but you must participate in connecting what you're learning in school to your own life and future. This requires thought and effort (important parts of mastery goals). Research shows that usefulness and interest are connected.[32] Therefore, always try to relate new information to your personal experience.

Sometimes the connections won't be obvious. Don't dismiss an idea or topic as irrelevant or stupid just because you can't see the relevance in the moment. For example, I didn't fully realize the power of metaphors (i.e., comparing two dissimilar things to show they do have something in common) when I first learned about them in high school English class. But, ten years later when I was counseling people, metaphors became very useful. I am glad I didn't dismiss them as useless. I'll give you a great example of a metaphor in Key #7.

SUGGESTION #2: I try very hard to capture my students' interest. Once I have their interest, I try to help them stay interested. However, I cannot "make" interest happen. Participating in class is a great way to develop and maintain your interest.[34] For example, when the teacher asks questions during class, try to answer them. Also ask your own questions during class. This is a way to develop a mastery orientation. Mastery-oriented students want "meaning," not just the answers for the test. This will also help you develop more sophisticated epistemological beliefs (Key #1).

SUGGESTION #3: Research by Roger Azevedo suggested that you will be better able to generate interest if you have enough time to do things and if you feel competent.[35] Many students these days have obligations outside of class. But it is hard to be interested in school if you are overwhelmed by all the other stuff you have to do. So, try your best to not overload yourself.

SUGGESTION #4: Your interest affects how much time you spend studying. In a series of three studies, Lisa Son and Janet Metcalfe found that students spend more time studying the things they find interesting.[36] However, just because you find something interesting and, therefore, study it more, doesn't necessarily mean it is the most important material. Study everything! Study everything thoroughly.

FINAL THOUGHTS

I certainly hope my explanations and examples helped you understand the different types of goals. Pause for a moment and think about what you are learning and how it relates to you (apply suggestion #1). Please also consider that, in college (and life), you will have many goals, and certain goals will take priority over others at different times.[37] Our goals, interests, and circumstances change and evolve over time.

Now you are ready to learn about the importance of confidence in your abilities. In psychology, we refer to that as self-efficacy, and it is Key #4.

KEY #4 - SELF-EFFICACY

Confidence in your abilities influences how you perceive your past and future. It can bolster your motivation, effort, and chances for success.

Self-efficacy is psychology's term for the confidence you have in your ability to accomplish something. It is a belief in your own competence. So, are you pretty confident in your cooking ability? How about playing baseball? Maybe you are confident in your ability to make new friends or give a speech.

Let's focus specifically on school success. In what school-related abilities do you have confidence? Math? Physics? Art? History? Anatomy? Social studies? Computer programming? Economics? Languages? Do you have confidence in specific skills like taking notes, doing a research paper, organization, time management, and reading comprehension? Do you have a good vocabulary? How is your grammar?

Teachers, tutors, and other books have a lot to say about studying and academic skills. But how effective will those skills be if you lack confidence in your ability to use them?

Why is Self-efficacy Important?

How well you do, how hard you try, your choice of tasks, and your expectations and values are all influenced by your confidence.[1] If you hold stronger beliefs about your ability, you are more likely to set higher goals for achievement, which can, in turn, increase your effort and persistence.[2,3]

Confidence in your ability is a great source of motivation.[4] Students with greater academic self-efficacy are more likely to be engaged in an activity, persist, recover when things go poorly, and achieve their goals at a higher level than students with lower levels of self-efficacy.[5,6,7] In 1994, Albert Bandura stated "beliefs of personal efficacy can shape the course [of a person's life] by influencing the types of activities and environments" he/she chooses.[8]

In terms of what you are learning in this book, believing that "academic success is under [your] control" represents a growth mindset and more effective attributions, and is a significant step toward becoming a self-regulated learner.[9] You will learn about self-regulated learning in this book too. It is Key #6.

Self-efficacy: It Depends

As you might have guessed, you can have a different level of confidence in everything from grammar to graduation. Self-efficacy depends on the situation, topic, or skill you consider. As a personal example, I lack confidence in my ability to do complicated math, but if you give me a presentation to do, I have a lot of confidence in my ability. The funny thing is that confidence in your ability and your actual ability can be very different. Truthfully, although I don't have a lot of math efficacy, I got A's in math throughout high school and college. And, just because I have confidence in my ability to do a presentation doesn't mean I'm the best at it.

Self-efficacy increases your academic performance and your persistence.[10] In a 2004 review, out of 9 possible factors, academic self-efficacy was the best predictor of GPA![11] Clearly, academic self-efficacy is extremely important. This exemplifies that how *you think* can affect your grades.

Self-efficacy: The Work of Albert Bandura

In 1977, Albert Bandura wrote a paper that stimulated decades of research about self-efficacy and motivation. Bandura described an efficacy expectation as "the conviction that [a person] can successfully execute the behavior required to produce the [desired] outcomes."[12] With efficacy, I am talking about your belief that you can do a behavior (whether it gets you the result you want or not). Many students are confident that they can get a high GPA but fail to do so. Others lack confidence in their academic ability when they may, in fact, do very well in school.

Albert Bandura explained that self-efficacy comes from four sources. I have added school-related examples to help you apply the four sources to your own experience.

Source 1: Experience

The first source of self-efficacy comes from your actual experiences. Let's say you write, for the very first time, a poem in a creative writing class. You receive a good grade, and the teacher tells the class how good your poem is. As you write more poems, you continue to get positive feedback and good grades. You are having success. That success will increase the confidence you have in your creative writing ability.

Now assume the opposite is happening in your architectural drafting class. You are getting low grades and negative feedback on your designs and drawings. Over time, these "failures" may reduce your sense of efficacy. Because writing poems and drawing schematics are different skills, you will probably develop high self-efficacy for creative writing and simultaneously hold low efficacy beliefs for architectural drafting.

As explained by Bandura, "successes raise mastery expectations; repeated failures lower them," and repeated successes reduce the "negative impact of occasional failures."[13] Other researchers wrote, "before…students can begin to think about school learning playing a realistic role in their futures, they must begin experiencing consistent and meaningful success in school."[14]

Sometimes feelings of confidence can spill over (i.e., generalize) to other settings and activities. High self-efficacy for creative writing might spill over to writing research papers and short stories, but it might not. There are many factors that contribute to how specific or general self-efficacy becomes based on learning experiences (too many to consider in this book). Simply remember that you can have different levels of efficacy for different school subjects, assignments, and activities.

There is an important link between your previous experiences, your self-efficacy, and your goals. That link is Key #2, attributions. Bernard Weiner explained that your confidence and future goals are based much more on how you perceive your past experiences than the actual experiences themselves.[15] For example, if you did well in high school but attribute your success to luck, you may still lack confidence in your ability. As such, you might set lower academic goals in college or worry a lot about doing poorly.

Source 2: Vicarious Experience

The second source of self-efficacy information comes from "vicarious experiences." Sometimes confidence in your ability increases or decreases based solely on seeing someone else do a behavior. For example, if you observe a classmate build a model of a house using popsicle sticks (something you've never done before), you might suddenly feel confident that you can do it too. Your feeling of confidence is not based on your own experience; it is based on what someone else did and experienced. Here's another example. Have you ever watched someone do a presentation and screw it up? Have you ever felt nervous or embarrassed for the person? You weren't doing the presentation so why did you feel nervous or embarrassed? Both are examples of vicarious experiences.

Consider the example of doing a presentation. Feeling nervous about giving a presentation is common for many students. However, you can develop confidence in your ability to do a presentation by watching other students successfully complete them. This is not as powerful as successfully doing a presentation yourself but it can help. This is part of how teaching and tutoring can be helpful; watching someone else succeed can help us build feelings of confidence. If you see someone else perform a behavior and think, "I can do that too," your efficacy can increase even though you haven't tried the behavior yourself. Albert Bandura suggested that seeing many different people with many different skill levels try something and succeed is more beneficial than simply watching the teacher do it.[16,17] So, observe your classmates and friends. Pay attention to what works for them. You might find yourself feeling more confident that you can do those things too.

Source 3: Persuasion

The third source of self-efficacy comes from verbal persuasion. Sometimes a bit of encouragement from someone you trust, love, or respect is enough to give you a little more confidence. Think of a person in your life who you might believe if she said to you, "I know you can do it. You'll be great." Maybe that person is a parent or a teacher. Do you remember a time when you doubted your ability and a coach or a friend or a teacher gently encouraged you and you felt a little more confident? Have you ever done that for one of your friends or a family member? This is also not as powerful an influence on self-efficacy as succeeding at something, but it can work wonders at times. For me, my mother has been a never-ending source of encouragement in everything I have done. Her support has helped me overcome fears and helped me achieve a lot of personal goals. (I love you, Mom!)

Source 4: Emotion

The fourth source of self-efficacy is your level of emotional arousal. In the face of a challenging task, such as a tough assignment, a presentation, or an important exam, you interpret your level of internal arousal as a cue about your confidence and skill. For example, if you feel really nervous, you might think you lack skill or knowledge. That interpretation lowers your confidence. Alternatively, if you feel pretty calm (i.e., low arousal), you are more likely to interpret that as a sign of confidence.

Think of how this relates to Key #2, attributions. If you attribute your nervousness to a normal part of taking an exam, you probably won't worry as much. If, however, you attribute your nervousness to "I suck at taking tests," you will have low feelings of efficacy and will worry a lot during the exam. That is very distracting and lowers your performance.

Self-efficacy: Your Thoughts, Motivation, Emotions, and Choices

Self-efficacy influences your thinking, motivation, feelings, and the choices you make.[18] These are all part of your school experience. To make it clear how your sense of efficacy influences these areas of your life, let's begin with a familiar scenario: It is the beginning of the semester and you are choosing your classes. One of the classes is something you have never taken before – psychology.

Thoughts

How does your sense of efficacy affect your thinking? For starters, it affects **how you think** about learning and school. Do you remember the first Psychological Key to Student Success? That's right, efficacy influences your mindset about intelligence and whether it is fixed or changeable. It also influences how you set and pursue goals. Yes, that is Key #3. If you have more confidence, you are likely to set and pursue better goals, such as mastering what you study. If you lack confidence, you may think you aren't capable and, therefore, set lower goals and standards for yourself. Researchers have noted that if you believe you cannot reach a goal, you are less likely to pursue that goal. [19] Your beliefs (Key #1) are very powerful.

Self-efficacy also influences thoughts about the future. It is tough to imagine success in school if you lack confidence in academics. If you have experienced a lot of previous academic success, however, you are more likely to feel confident in your abilities and expect future successes.

Motivation

Self-efficacy is related to motivation based on how you make attributions (Key #2). Students who have higher self-efficacy are more likely to "work harder, persist, and eventually achieve at higher levels."[20] For example, if you are struggling, high self-efficacy can lead you to attribute the difficulties to lack of effort. In response, you will increase effort. That fits with the growth mindset. However, in the same situation but with low self-efficacy, the attribution may be that you are stupid or incapable. That may lead you to give up because you believe you can't do it (regardless of effort). That fits with the fixed mindset.

SUGGESTION #1: As explained above, having success experiences is the best way to build confidence and increase motivation. In school, many of the things you need to accomplish are based on skills such as time management, goal-setting, and prioritizing. These are skills that make academic tasks easier, especially when you have all of them. I will give you time management tips later in the book. Spend time developing these skills and you will become more confident managing and successfully completing academic tasks. This requires effort on your part. What are you prepared to do?

SUGGESTION #2: One way to increase motivation and self-efficacy relates to goals (Key #3). When you are first learning something, you can increase motivation and self-efficacy by setting proximal goals (i.e., smaller, short-term) with specific performance expectations (i.e., behaviors you will do).[21] That is, break tasks into smaller parts and then say exactly what parts you will do, and when. As your skills and knowledge increase, setting more challenging goals will increase your motivation and self-efficacy.

For example, when you first start learning a type of math, set a goal that you will complete two practice problems each night. As you get better at the problems, you can select more challenging problems to practice each night. Basically, I am telling you to start small and build up over time. Again, this requires effort. What are you prepared to do?

SUGGESTION #3: Actively asking for feedback about how you are doing is an important skill. That's right. *Asking for feedback and help is a skill*. When you ask teachers for feedback, or when you seek clarification about feedback you already got, ask them for specific ideas and advice.

Don't just ask about why an answer is right or wrong. Develop a mastery approach (Key #3) by telling your teacher *how* you did the assignment or *how* you studied for an exam. Then ask how she would have done it. Ask for specific ideas about what strategies you can use. If there is a learning or tutoring center at your school, that's another great place to get suggestions. Tutors and teachers can model good strategies for you (that is an example of increasing your self-efficacy through vicarious experience).

Getting feedback on the strategies you used has been shown to increase self-efficacy.[22] Support and encouragement can increase your confidence best when they relate to improving your performance through strategy suggestions.[23] Make sure you talk to your teachers about this. This also requires effort. What are you prepared to do?

SUGGESTION #4: Find teachers and peers who have studying and thinking habits that promote deep learning. Pay close attention to how your teachers think about topics and how they solve problems. Observe (and ask directly about) how successful friends and classmates tackle difficult assignments. How do they approach studying? Teachers and some of your peers can be excellent models from whom you can learn more effective studying and thinking strategies. This can enhance your academic self-efficacy as you practice the

effective strategies used by those people.[24]
This requires effort. What are you prepared
to do?

Emotions

The third area affected by your efficacy is feelings. If you experience a lot of self-doubt, how do you feel? Most feel worried. They are afraid of failure. They are afraid of looking stupid. They are afraid to even try, so they avoid anything challenging. How can you succeed at the college level if you avoid challenges? Does that sound familiar? We talked about that when we considered performance-avoidance goals in Key #3. Fear often lowers performance. So, in college, low self-efficacy can set you up to fail, not because you lack skill, but because you don't believe you can do it, feel afraid of failure, and therefore don't try (or don't try hard enough).

What about the positive side? Higher self-efficacy leaves you feeling confident. When challenges arise, you don't feel fear; you feel motivated. You see an opportunity, not a threat. As a result, you dive in and set about achieving whatever it is that needs to be done. In that way, your feelings play a "major guiding and regulatory role in [your] cognitive and motivational systems."[25] That means self-efficacy gives you positive feelings, better thoughts, and more motivation. This all fits with perceived academic control, persistence, resilience, motivation, the growth mindset, internal and controllable attributions, and mastery goals. That is pretty much everything you've read about so far!

SUGGESTION: Learning to monitor and control emotions is something that is a challenge during adolescence but is a struggle that many experience into adulthood as well.[26] Taking care of yourself, tending to your mental health, and developing self-awareness will help you be a more effective and successful student. You need to pay attention to your emotions, what leads to them, and how to effectively manage them. Emotions can be a great source of motivation. Reading this book is a step toward higher self-awareness, healthier emotions, greater confidence, and better academic achievement. (And thank you for letting me help you.)

Choices

The fourth area that self-efficacy influences is the choices you make. Think about the courses you choose. Not all of them are required; some are electives. How do you choose? Are your choices based on interest? Do you look at the course requirements and compare that with your perceived abilities? Confidence in your abilities will probably influence your choice of major and eventual career, not just elective classes.

Efficacy influences decisions to do or not do certain things in school. If you lack confidence in your abilities, you are less likely to try something. But if you have high self-efficacy, you are more likely to take on a new challenge. Students with higher self-efficacy due to previous success are more likely to adopt approach goals.[27] We considered the benefits of approach goals, compared to avoidance goals, in Key #3. Improving self-regulation (you will read about this in Key #6) can increase confidence in abilities, which, in turn, increases job attendance.[28]

Increasing Your Self-efficacy

In addition to the many suggestions you have read so far, here are some more tips for improving your academic confidence:[29]

- Set clear goals for homework and studying *every day*.

- Before you begin today's work, review the homework and studying goals you accomplished the previous day.

- Think about what you have learned or become better at over the past week or month. Do this every week/month. Remind and show yourself that you are improving.

- Develop a growth mindset. Remember, treat everything in school like it is a skill you can improve with effort and practice.

- Attribute setbacks to internal, controllable, and unstable factors like concentration and effort.

- Break all tasks into small, manageable goals.

- Observe and model the behavior of people who have school skills you admire. You can learn those skills too.

FINAL THOUGHTS

Confidence in school-related abilities is important to your level of achievement. It influences your thoughts, motivation, emotions, and choices. Essentially, it is a type of belief. Because of the strong influence self-efficacy can have, it is worthwhile for you to consider. I suggest that you discuss your level of confidence with your professors. They can help you build academic efficacy by teaching you skills and offering advice. That kind of tutoring can be very helpful.

The next Key is another great example of learning **how to think**. It has a crazy name – metacognition.

KEY #5 – METACOGNITION

Metacognition is a set of thinking skills that will help you know how and when to use certain studying skills, making your studying more effective and efficient.

In 1997 the American Psychological Association "highlighted metacognition as one of the more important factors in contributing towards effective learning."[1] That makes me curious. If it is so important, why do so few teachers talk about it? Have teachers ever mentioned it to you? Until now, have you ever heard of metacognition?

In 1979, developmental psychologist John Flavell coined the term "metacognition." He defined it as ***"thinking about thinking."***[2] Metacognition is an awareness of your own thinking and how that can help you develop better learning strategies.[3] Regulating your own learning involves knowing what thinking strategies work and analyzing your thinking habits.[4] Metacognition also includes how you "manage the internal aspects of learning."[5]

Yes, I know. These academic-sounding terms and quotations can be painful. Welcome to my world! Essentially, metacognition is your awareness of how helpful or hurtful your thoughts are as you do homework, study, and complete exams. Metacognition allows you to think about, understand, and control your learning.[6] It is very important to you because it allows you to plan your studying, select appropriate studying strategies, estimate how well you are doing, and adjust your strategies to ensure you get the results you want.[7] Awareness of your thoughts is critical to having self-control when you study.

Metacognitive Knowledge, Experiences, and Skills

In 2011, a university professor named Anastasia Efklides (pronounced Eff-klee-dees) published an article that explained interesting details about metacognition. Metacognition is more than just an awareness of your own thinking. Efklides asserted that metacognition is made up of three things: metacognitive knowledge, metacognitive experiences, and metacognitive skills.[8] Let's see how these concepts will help you succeed in college.

Metacognitive Knowledge – How to Think

Metacognitive knowledge includes the awareness you have of your strengths and weaknesses as a learner and your *beliefs* about learning (Key #1), your style of making *attributions* (Key #2), and your *goals* (Key #3). Guess what – I have been trying to build your metacognitive knowledge from the start of this book! The more you know about your own beliefs, attributions, and goals, the more metacognitive knowledge you have.

Metacognitive knowledge also includes what you know about effective thinking processes (e.g., about how memory works and about different learning strategies and how to use them). It further includes your general level of self-awareness (something I'm trying to help you increase with this book). The purpose of metacognitive knowledge is to help you plan, strategize, and understand your studying efforts.[9]

Metacognitive Experiences – Your Feelings and Reactions

Metacognitive experiences include your awareness of a task and the processing of information related to it. For example, right now you are aware that you are reading this book and trying to understand what it means. You are aware of whether you are "getting it" or if you are confused.

Metacognitive experiences include the feelings of familiarity, knowing, and difficulty you experience when you are studying. For example, when you're reading something and think, "Hey, I've heard of that before," that is the feeling of familiarity. As you are listening to a lecture and think, "Ya, I knew that already," that is the feeling of knowing. If you are studying something over and over and think, "I just don't get it," that is the feeling of difficulty.

Remember self-efficacy (Key #4)? Your level of confidence influences how easy or difficult learning feels. For example, a thought such as "I suck at this" might go with the feeling of difficulty whereas "I know I can figure this out" might be a thought you have when you are reading something complicated in a textbook.

Metacognitive Skills - Regulating Your Own Thinking

Metacognitive skills are strategies used to control your thinking. They are *not* simple studying skills. Studying skills are basic tools. Metacognitive skills are *thinking strategies* that help you know how and when to use certain studying skills.

Efklides explained that our metacognitive experiences, such as the feeling of difficulty, activate the metacognitive skills we use to regulate our thinking about the task.[10] Basically, you can develop skills to control your thoughts when you have the feeling of difficulty. Even something as simple as telling yourself, "Concentrate," is a metacognitive skill. Telling yourself that "mistakes are natural and OK" is a metacognitive skill. Telling yourself, "I did a good job," when you complete your homework is a metacognitive skill. Successful students use more of these skills compared to less successful students.[11]

An Example: The Feeling of Difficulty

The feeling of difficulty is one of the most important metacognitive experiences students have, and no one ever tells you about it. Teachers don't mention this when they talk about studying skills. This is probably because it is not the same as taking notes, reviewing, or making flashcards, so it might not seem like an academic skill. But I wrote this book because *how you think* is extremely important. Are you convinced yet? Are you a believer?

Sometimes studying does not go smoothly. Maybe you are taking a tough class. As you work on the practice problems, you might struggle to figure out how to solve them. Maybe you think, "I don't get it. This is too hard," as you work on some chemistry problems or a paper for your English class. Everyone has these experiences... students, parents, managers, lawyers, engineers, and even teachers. The feeling of difficulty occurs when thinking and learning is hard.

Can you think of a time when you experienced the feeling of difficulty? How did you feel? What did you do? How did it affect your motivation?

The feeling of difficulty can be a good thing or a bad thing. *It all depends on the attribution you make* (Key #2). Remember that an attribution is your explanation for why things happen. When you attribute the feeling of difficulty to a lack of ability (i.e., "I'm stupid"), you are more likely to give up. If you attribute the feeling of difficulty to the task being hard or your need to try harder, you are more likely to keep trying.

When you have the feeling of difficulty you must figure out the source of the problem, why the problem exists, and what you can do about it. If you believe that task difficulty is responsible for your problem, you have to evaluate why it seems hard. Maybe you attribute the difficulty to the fact you are lacking information. That attribution is external and controllable. The problem (needing information) exists outside of you but is something you can fix by referring to your notes, re-reading the instructions, or jumping online to look up an article. In this case, you will be motivated to find what you need and then continue with the task. The feeling of difficulty will be replaced by a new metacognitive experience called a feeling of confidence. You suddenly feel like everything will get sorted out and you anticipate success. What is surprising (and neat) is how quickly and almost automatically that metacognitive analysis happens in your mind. But recognizing and understanding these quick and seemingly automatic thoughts is important.

Here's another possibility. What might happen if you believe the problem is, well, you? Maybe the quick and seemingly automatic analysis yields the thought, "I'm stupid." That attribution is internal, stable, and uncontrollable. It is something inside you that can't be changed quickly. Now you are stuck. As soon as that attribution is made, you might feel frustrated, worried, or defeated. These attribution-dependent emotions make you want to avoid the source of the problem, which is actually yourself. Because you cannot crawl out of your own skin, and because you cannot instantly get smarter, you are motivated to avoid the task. So, you put it away and the frustration and anxiety go away temporarily. But hours or days later the difficult, unfinished task is still lurking and the anxiety returns. That fear of failure is more common for students with performance-avoidance goals (Key #3) and low self-efficacy (Key #4).

The more you put things off, the more likely you are to make the failure come true. Let me say that again. The more you put things off, the more likely you are to create failure. How is your motivation for school now? The worst part is that the "I'm stupid" attribution is usually *wrong*. You basically imagine yourself into a failure that was completely avoidable. Have I mentioned that **how you think** is important?

The Importance of Metacognition

People tend to have consistent ways of thinking. Do you tend to give up or keep trying when something is hard? Maybe you put things off and justify your procrastination with, "I just need a little break." This is a crucial aspect of your thinking that will dramatically affect your studying, far more even than your actual knowledge or ability.

All of the Psychological Keys we have considered so far are part of your metacognitive knowledge and can be used as metacognitive skills once you master them. That's right. Everything you have learned about motivation, beliefs, attributions, achievement goals and interest, and self-efficacy are now part of your metacognitive knowledge. Soon, even the ideas about metacognition will be part of your metacognitive knowledge.

In 2002, educational psychologist Paul Pintrich advised that educators should teach metacognitive knowledge to students explicitly.[12] He thought teachers should tell students about metacognition. As you might have guessed, I totally agree. I am trying hard to help you improve your metacognitive knowledge and skills. My book is designed to clearly point out the importance of beliefs, attributions, goals and interest, self-efficacy, metacognition, self-regulation, thinking errors, and culture and how they relate to your success as a student. They are the Psychological Keys to Student Success. These psychological concepts go above and beyond simple studying strategies.

Without these personal and thinking skills, studying skills will only take you so far. Study strategies are weaker without increasing self-awareness first. The Dunning-Kruger effect says that if you lack a skill, you will make mistakes *and* be unaware that you are making those mistakes.[13] Many students who lack metacognitive knowledge and skills don't realize it and, therefore, never figure out why their studying strategies are not working.

Developing Your Metacognitive Skills

Biology professor Kimberly Tanner wrote an article about how teachers can help students become more aware of and effectively utilize metacognition in their studying.[14] Based on research, Tanner made a list of questions that students can ask themselves to become stronger in the metacognitive aspects of studying and learning.

Tanner's article is a treasure trove of great of questions you can ask yourself that will focus and guide your learning. These questions give you practice being more self-aware and intentional when it comes to learning. These questions can help you plan, monitor, and evaluate your learning.

Here are some specific examples. Before you attend a lecture or read a chapter in a book, ask yourself, "What do I already know about this topic?" This encourages you to analyze your own thoughts about a topic. During a lecture ask yourself, "What concepts are unclear? What is difficult?" It is *totally normal* to be confused. Do not avoid it – embrace confusion. As you are studying, write down questions you have and confusion you are experiencing. The confusion you feel and questions you are silently thinking about are examples of meta-cognitive experiences. You must think about your understanding (or lack thereof). That is thinking about thinking. In that moment, you are practicing metacognition.

Metacognitive Skills for Homework - Suggestions

When you're doing homework, you can use metacognition to help you plan, monitor, and evaluate your work.

Before you begin, ask yourself what material and resources you need to successfully meet the goals and expectations. Make sure you carefully read the instructions (I don't like it when I have to give you a bad grade because you didn't follow directions). Estimate how much time you need. Remember to break tasks into smaller goals. Think about previous assignments you've done and how you might make this one better. Think about your skills and focus on improvement (growth mindset).

During the assignment (i.e., as you are doing it), keep track of how you are doing. Keep track of what strategies are working and which ones are not. Be aware of what is challenging and confusing. Ask yourself again about resources you could find that will clear up any confusion or difficulty you are having. Do you need to Google something? Should you find a resource in the textbook or your library's online databases? Maybe you should email the teacher and ask a question or two.

After you complete the homework, evaluate how you did. Compare the instructions, goals, and expectations given in the assignment with what you have produced. Here's a great thing to try: As best you can, pretend to be the teacher. What will your teacher or prof like about your work? What criticisms can you anticipate? Anticipating criticism is often related to the confusions you experienced, the sections you rushed through, the resources you did not use, things you chose to not look up or double-check, etc. If you feel like something isn't very good, *fix it* by proofreading, editing, and having some pride. Remember, you are putting your name on this. That should mean something to you.

Metacognitive Skills for Exams - Suggestions

When we considered Key #1, Beliefs & Mindset, I explained that your beliefs about the type of exam will influence how you study for it. *Before* an exam, think about all the different ways the teacher could ask questions, regardless of the type of exam. Think about how challenging she could make multiple-choice questions. Remember that even what you think is an "easy" exam format could, in fact, be challenging. If I wanted to, I could totally kill you on a multiple-choice exam – but I don't do that.

Further challenge your beliefs with this: A lot of college professors use multiple-choice exam questions that are examples of concepts even though they didn't use those particular examples in class. So, a great metacognitive skill is studying all concepts like you will have to apply them (by the way, if the prof does give examples in class, make sure you write them down). I will teach you more about exam questions and how to study for them in the Incredibly Awesome Learning Strategies section of this book. You will love it. I will tell you how professors like me make questions so you can study properly for them.

Lev Vygotsky, a famous developmental psychologist, observed that young children talk to themselves as they do an activity. They narrate what they are doing and why. If you have kids (or work with them), you have probably seen this. It is adorable! Vygotsky called this "private speech." It is an obvious example of being aware of your own thoughts. Here's the tip (try this when you are working on a problem or trying to learn something difficult): Think out loud. This is *not* the same as reading out loud. I'm saying you should express your feelings of familiarity, knowing, and difficulty about what you are reading or working on. For example, "The order of operations in math says I have to multiply things before I do addition." By doing this, you force yourself to be aware of your own thought processes. This is a metacognitive skill.

Another great metacognitive exercise can be done *after* an exam. Think about what strategies you used to study. Did you read and re-read the material? If so, how many times? Did you use flash-cards? Did you re-write or summarize your notes? Did you highlight the book? Did you attend a study group? Did you test yourself? After you analyze the basic studying strategies you used, how much actual time did you spend studying?

Here's the interesting part. How did you do on the exam? Did your studying strategies prepare you well and give you the results you wanted? Based on that analysis, you have to think, "How will I study for the next exam?"

Gregory Schraw described what he called a "strategy evaluation matrix."[15] It is a chart that lists cognitive and studying strategies you can use plus information about how, when, and why to use the strategy. The chart has four columns: strategy, how to use, when to use, and why to use. It will have as many rows as you have studying and thinking strategies.

Here is an example that Schraw gave in his work. Consider "skimming" as a strategy. In the *how to use* column, he suggested that with this strategy you search for headings, highlighted words, and summaries. In the *when to use* column he suggested that skimming be used prior to reading the chapter in detail. In the *why to use* column he suggested that skimming gives you a conceptual overview and that it will help focus your attention.

You should make your own chart and fill in the details (see example below). By doing that, you will identify metacognitive and self-regulated learning (Key #6, coming up next) strategies. This is an awesome exercise. For example, let's say you highlight passages in a textbook as you read. Once you list the strategy, you should figure out how, when, and why you use the strategy. This requires you to examine your thoughts about the strategy. *That* is an exercise in metacognition. Another strategy is re-reading. How, when, and why do you use it? If you use flashcards, fill in the how, when, and why columns. Do you self-test? How, when, and why?

Strategy	How to use	When to use	Why to use
Skimming	Look for headings, highlighted words, and summaries	Prior to reading the chapter in detail	Gives a conceptual overview; helps me focus my attention
Highlighting			
Re-reading			
Self-testing			

Metacognition's Relationship to Keys #1 and 4

Consider the relationship between your beliefs about yourself as a student (Key #1 – Beliefs & Mindset) and metacognition. You came (or will come) to college with beliefs about your own academic ability. These beliefs are part of your metacognitive knowledge. For example, how do you define yourself as a student? Are you a "good" student (by the way, what does that actually mean)? Are you a "hard worker?" Are you "lazy?" Do you "suck?" Are you "good enough?" These ideas influence your approach to homework, assignments, and exams.

Let's say you believe you are a good student because you got A's and B's in high school. You are confident when you start college, choose your classes, and work on assignments. What will happen if classes are harder than you expected? What thoughts will you have when you don't understand something? What feelings will you be aware of in that instant? Your awareness of those thoughts and feelings are metacognitive experiences.

Now imagine you arrive at college full of self-doubt (low self-efficacy). What thoughts and feelings will you have about classes and assignments? How will those thoughts and feelings affect your motivation and effort? You need to understand metacognition because it directly influences your motivation.

Metacognition affects your performance before, during, and after you do an assignment. Before you start an assignment, you will think about your existing knowledge and compare that with what you need to know to successfully complete the assignment. As you do an assignment, and it is tough, you might doubt your ability. After the assignment is submitted, getting a good grade will bolster your confidence and fuel positive thoughts and feelings about your ability.

However, negative feedback might shake your confidence. Do you see how metacognition works before, during, and after an assignment?

As a college prof, I want to help weaker students become more skilled and confident, and help the already-strong students be even more skilled. Another important part of my job is evaluating whether the beliefs you have about your abilities are accurate or not. I know a lot of students who got A's in high school and, therefore, believe they are good students. However, if they lack academic (e.g., reading and writing) and personal (e.g., perceived academic control, resilience, persistence, growth mindset, etc.) skills, they may have difficulties in college. Alternatively, I have met students who have had negative experiences in school prior to college who are very insightful, intelligent, and skilled.

Both cases are unfortunate. Students who believe they are more skilled than they actually are experience surprise, anger, and frustration when they get negative feedback. As such, some do not believe the feedback, blame their instructors, and drop classes. Rather than trying to get better, they quit. On the other hand, students who are capable but don't believe in themselves may be afraid of failure and, in the face of any challenge, doubt themselves so much that they quit too. For teachers, both types of students require attention. We must maintain high standards (college is referred to as "higher education" for a reason) while encouraging and motivating students to stick with it.

Teachers can't *make* you change your thoughts. You need to be aware of your metacognitive knowledge and metacognitive experiences. You need to understand how they influence your motivation and perception of school. Then you can use them to your advantage. This kind of self-monitoring is a difficult but important metacognitive skill for academic and personal success.

Metacognition and Your Feelings and Motivation

Efklides suggested that metacognition also helps us understand the link between feelings and academic motivation.[16] When you are working on a task, you may experience intrinsic motivation, the kind of motivation when you are interested in something. This is usually accompanied by pleasant feelings. Together, that motivation and those pleasant feelings are a positive metacognitive experience. In that case, the result can be more focus, desire to complete the task, and persistence.

Conversely, if a task seems boring or irrelevant, you may have to rely on extrinsic motivation (such as wanting a high grade) to get through the task. Feelings such as boredom, disinterest, and annoyance are an unpleasant metacognitive experience. In this case, you may think to yourself, "Why bother," or "What's the point?" Such thoughts can reduce your motivation.

When you're doing an assignment and have previous knowledge or experience, you may have the feeling of familiarity or even a feeling of knowing. This can make the material seem easy. In psychology, we would say that you are experiencing high "perceptual fluency." That is a fancy way of saying that you are understanding the information easily. High perceptual fluency inspires confidence and motivation. Sometimes, however, the assignment will require you to think harder because you don't know anything about it. Having to think harder (i.e., low perceptual fluency) will make you consider that the task is complex, difficult, or new to you. For students with a growth mindset and mastery goals, this stimulates curiosity and effort. For others, this creates anxiety. Either way, pay attention to these feelings (which are metacognitive experiences) and how they affect your motivation.

FINAL THOUGHTS

Metacognition is a type of advanced thinking skill. It will help you use studying strategies effectively and increase persistence when studying is difficult.[17] Metacognition is a key component of self-regulated learning[18] which is the next Psychological Key to Student Success.

I cannot be there with you right now but I know you are doing a great job. If you are starting to see that the Psychological Keys to Student Success are all connected, you have made great progress!

KEY #6 – SELF-REGULATED LEARNING

Being successful in school is not as much about ability as it is responsibility. Self-control is part of your academic success.

May I offer you and nice, freshly baked chocolate chip cookie? Does that sound good? How about a radish? Which would you prefer?

In 1998, researchers presented 67 university students (who had not eaten in three hours) with a stack of freshly baked chocolate chip cookies and a bowl of radishes.[1] Some of the students were instructed to eat two or three of the cookies but not the radishes. Other students were told to eat two or three of the radishes but none of the cookies. The experimenters left the room and secretly observed the students through a one-way mirror for five minutes. If you were in the radish group, would you cheat and eat a cookie or could you resist the temptation?

The experimenters observed that those who were instructed to eat only radishes had a hard time resisting the cookies, but they successfully avoided the temptation. After five minutes, the experimenters returned and gave all the students problems to solve. The students did not know the problems were impossible (there was no solution).

The researchers discovered something very interesting. The students who were allowed to eat the cookies persisted in trying to solve the impossible problems, on average, for over 18 minutes. The students who had resisted eating the cookies gave up trying to solve the problems, on average, after only 8 minutes. Using their "willpower" to resist the cookies tired them out!

Self-control is a bit like a muscle. When we use self-control, the muscle gets tired (and it seems like temptations get stronger). Please keep that in mind the next time you leave studying for the end of a long day. You're much more likely to "give in" and watch TV than you are to study for hours, despite your best intentions. With training, however, the more we use our self-control, the stronger it gets.

With this sixth Psychological Key to Student Success, my goal is to help you work out and strengthen your self-control muscles. Self-control is a necessary personal skill to succeed in college.[2] It is not your parents' or your professors' responsibility to remind you to read, study, and complete assignments.

I strongly recommend you re-read that last paragraph…twice. Ok, you should highlight it too. Now memorize it and text it to all your friends. Tweet it. Get personalized license plates (SELFCTRL). Most importantly, go tell your parents and teachers you understand that reading, studying, and completing assignments are *your responsibility*. They'll be thrilled to know you get it. With this book, I am trying to help you meet this responsibility, meet it well, and meet it consistently.

Unfortunately, many high school teachers and college professors impose too much structure and control over your schoolwork. That is a mistake.[3] Why is it a mistake? The answer lies in a simple behavioral principle: the more they do, the less you have to. We need to teach you how to control yourself, motivate yourself, and direct yourself.

For example, high school students need to learn how to turn homework assignments into personal goals, how to set aside study time, how to make sure they complete their goals, and how to antic-ipate the consequences for the decisions they make.[4] Those are skills necessary in college.

In a nutshell, self-regulated learning (SRL) is about motivating yourself, setting goals, achieving your goals, evaluating your per-formance, and learning from that process. It is a "dynamic process involving cognition, emotion, behavior, and context."[5] That means SRL is the interaction between your thoughts, feelings, actions, and surroundings. SRL will help you control your studying and learn-ing better. It will also help you build academic self-efficacy, increase thinking strategies, and learn more deeply.[6]

There are many theories of SRL.[7] No matter which one you read, it will say that SRL deals with metacognitive skills such as planning, monitoring, and evaluating your work. SRL also includes metacognitive skills and motivational strategies, such as modifying your beliefs, making better attributions, and managing your own emotions.[8] Can you see how we have already been working on this stuff? We've been working on building up your self-regulated learn-ing muscles all along!

SRL is one of the Psychological Keys to Student Success because it mediates (i.e., helps explain) the relationship between you and your level of achievement.[9] Teaching you studying skills is only effective if it makes you aware of self-control strategies needed in specific learning situations.[10] In other words, you need SRL skills to make basic studying skills effective. In addition, self-regulation con-nects your academic goals and the quality of your efforts to achieve.[11]

On the flip side, students who lack academic self-regulatory skills often underachieve.[12] This helps explain why some really smart and capable students don't get good grades. They are academically strong but their lack of self-control prevents them from accomplish-ing as much as they could.

What Are Self-regulated Learners Like?

Barry Zimmerman described self-regulated learners as students who "find a way to succeed."[13] They actively seek out information, especially when something is unclear or confusing, and accept more responsibility for their own achievement. He wrote that self-regulated learners understand the link between self-control and their level of academic achievement. They understand the importance of self-reflection, self-assessment, and self-improvement.

Self-regulated learners are proactive; they seek out opportunities to learn and they do it long before assignments are due and exams are looming. Self-regulated learners adapt to changing conditions and don't lose sight of their goals when challenges arise.[14]

As you'll see throughout this chapter, SRL interacts with a number of the other Keys I've already described. For example, self-regulated learning skills lead to greater motivation and achievement.[15] Research has shown that students with self-efficacy for self-regulated learning get better grades.[16] That combines Key #4 with SRL. Research also suggests that students with mastery goals (Key #3) are more successful with SRL.[17]

Barry Zimmerman's Model of SRL

In 1998, Zimmerman explained that self-regulated learning involves "self-generated thoughts, feelings, and actions for attaining academic goals."[18] Essentially, this means that you need to direct your own thinking, feelings, and behavior as you try to achieve in school. It doesn't matter how small (read a few pages) or big (study for weeks) your goal is; you must control yourself to accomplish it.

According to Zimmerman, the six psychological dimensions of self-regulated learning are motivation, study strategies, time management, feedback, the environment, and other people.[19] I will describe each and offer practical suggestions for you.

1) Motivation

Motivation is the first dimension of Zimmerman's model of SRL and, as you'll recall, it is a chapter all by itself in the book you're reading. As a student, finding the drive to do a lot of reading and homework is challenging. What do you do when you just don't feel like studying or are bored with it? How do you make yourself study? You already read about motivation earlier in this book. Here is more educated advice about how to increase your motivation.

SUGGESTION #1: SRL is about planning, monitoring, and evaluating your work. Setting goals is part of the planning. Goals help you organize what you need to do, provide a source of motivation, and help you evaluate your progress. As such, goals are both a starting point and an end point.

I strongly recommend that, each day, you set goals for what school work you want to accomplish that day. This is like a to-do list. In my opinion, students sometimes think too far into the future. They try to think of what life will be like five years in the future and forget about the importance of short-term goals. There is a lot you need to accomplish *now* before you'll ever get to the five-year goal.

"Wait, Troy. Are you saying I shouldn't think about my future?"

No! But I want you to consider a slightly different perspective on your future. Thinking about your future is like looking at a map before you take a long road trip. You see yourself at the starting point and you measure how far it is to the destination. If you focus only on that distance, the trip may seem like it will take forever and you might get discouraged or frustrated. But, if you break that long road trip into smaller pieces, it feels much more manageable.

Getting through a semester, let alone getting all the way to graduation, can seem like a long time. So instead, focus on what you are going to accomplish *today*. Research has shown a relationship between higher achievement and students who set specific, proximal goals compared to setting distal goals.[20] A proximal goal is short-term and usually involves breaking a large task into a series of smaller tasks. Your academic achievement *today* is connected to the attainment of your future goals.[21]

Research shows that long-term goals are great motivators to get you started but short-term goals help you focus your attention and stay on task (part of SRL).[22] Having short-term goals gives you information and feedback *now*, which allows you to modify your strategies and make sure you are constantly on track for the longer-term goals.[23]

So, are you going to read part of a chapter? When? How many pages? Are you going to research information for that paper? Where are you going to look? How much time will you spend? Are you going to do some of those chemistry problems? When and how many? Set small goals *every* day. If you do, you will be amazed at how much you accomplish over the long term.

SUGGESTION #2: Top athletes visualize achieving their goals. They mentally "see" themselves performing tasks before they physically practice skills and before they compete. You can do this too. I have met many students who talk constantly about all the reasons they can't do homework on time or study enough for tests. They "see" their kids misbehaving, their jobs, their family obligations, etc. in their heads. This is bad visualization. They are visualizing reasons to not get things done. Of course, this makes school hard.

The good news is that you have a choice. Every moment, you can actively choose what you spend your time thinking about. Spend more time "seeing" yourself in the library reading after class instead of catching up on unimportant text messages – the "lol" and "wtf" can definitely wait. Imagine yourself sitting comfortably doing your homework after work instead of "vegging" in front of the television. Imagine yourself saying no (a psychological skill I'll describe later) to people who make too many requests for your time. Imagine telling them that school is *that* important to you (real friends and helpful family members will respect and support you).

This kind of visualization (called a "process simulation") can be an effective SRL strategy that can help eliminate negative learning beliefs (remember that beliefs are Key #1).[24] For example, one study showed that women who imagined success while pursuing their undergraduate degrees performed more successfully than those who imagined failure.[25] Don't just "dream." Think about *specific things you will do* to achieve your goals.

Motivational self-regulation is your effort "to produce favorable states of mind and positive outcomes, or prevent undesired events and unfavorable outcomes."[26] That means visualizing success includes your beliefs (Key #1), attributions (Key #2), achievement goals (Key #3), and planning (metacognitive skills in Key #5). Look at all those Psychological Keys to Student Success that are part of motivational self-regulation. This stuff is much cooler than just basic studying skills. You are becoming a more effective student and person!

SUGGESTION #3: As you know, self-efficacy (Key #4) is the confidence you have in your ability to accomplish something, and it varies depending on the situation. For example, I have more confidence learning things like psychology than things like architectural drafting (I'd make some messed-up buildings). In terms of school, what is your level of confidence for studying effectively?

In Key #4, we reviewed the sources of self-efficacy. The best way to build your studying self-efficacy is to practice the powerful learning strategies I describe later until you are good at them. It is easy to be confident when you have evidence that you are good at something. This confidence can increase motivation and improve the attributions you make.[27] In addition, self-efficacy can propel you to set more ambitious goals, persist when things are difficult, and increase your academic self-control (SRL).[28] So my suggestion is that you commit time to practicing academic skills. I am going to teach you Powerful Learning Strategies later.

SUGGESTION #4: You can use behavioral principles to reinforce good studying behavior. You can connect a treat or a break with the completion of a proximal goal. For example, you can promise yourself 10 minutes of texting *after* you finish reading 10 pages in the textbook. You can also give yourself verbal rewards any time (e.g., "I'm doing a good job."). Make sure you use positive self-talk. Encourage yourself. Encouragement, as you may recall, is a way to improve your self-efficacy (Key #4). You don't need someone else to encourage you. Oh, and by the way, positive self-talk is a metacognitive skill (Key #5).

SUGGESTION #5: Each time you read, study, or complete a homework assignment, remind yourself why it is important. Purposely think about why you enrolled in college in the first place. Make your homework and studying a reflection of your chances at getting a good job. Take one minute as you begin your schoolwork to reflect on this ultimate value. Notice how this relates to the visualizing I mentioned in Suggestion #2.

Your belief that a topic is interesting and important to your goals (Key #3) will help you be engaged and use good learning and study strategies.[29,30] Seeing how a class relates to your future connects you to the class and increases your motivation.

SUGGESTION #6: Christopher Wolters offered an idea I like very much. He called it "interest enhancement."[31] Do whatever you can to increase your enjoyment of each academic activity. When you are studying, for example, quiz yourself (an extremely powerful studying and metacognitive skill) and give yourself points for correct answers. Pretend you are on a game show. When you earn a certain number of points, you win a treat or a break (this is connected to Suggestion #5). If you read about something interesting, see if there's a cool YouTube video about it during one of your earned breaks and learn more about it. These are just a couple of examples. You can make up your own fun.

Please keep in mind that interest in a topic may require effort on your part. Your level of engagement influences your experience of interest (Key #3). In turn, your efforts to self-regulate interest can affect goals and their outcomes.[32] Basically, if you try to be interested you have a better chance of achieving at a higher level. Developing interest is related to intrinsic motivation and a willingness to make greater effort.[33] If you sit in class blaming everyone and everything else for your lack of interest (an example of a very unhealthy attribution), you will probably do poorly. Feeling helpless and blaming others trigger negative feelings that will distract you from your goals.[34]

2) Study Strategies

This is the second dimension of Zimmerman's model of SRL. So, what studying strategies do you have in your studying tool kit? How do you decide what strategy to use for your political science exam? How about your English exam? What strategies do you have for studying algebra? Art history? Biology? Welding techniques?

Studying strategies are like any other skill; they must be practiced before you will be good at them. Then you have to be able to select the appropriate strategy for any given topic or task. Developing the ability to select a good strategy is part of self-regulated learning. Awareness of what studying strategy will be most effective is a key metacognitive skill. For example, just because someone says using flash cards is great does not mean it will work for every test or class.

Zimmerman listed 14 self-regulated learning strategies. As you read this list, think about how many of these strategies have come up in our consideration of the Psychological Keys to Student Success. Here is Dr. Zimmerman's list: "self-evaluation, organization and transformation, goal setting and planning, information seeking, record keeping, self-monitoring, environmental structuring, giving self-consequences, rehearsing and memorizing, seeking social assistance, and reviewing."[35]

Later in this book you will read about powerful learning strategies as well as principles from educational psychology. If you take the time to learn and practice those strategies and principles, you will become a better and more efficient learner. Your confidence and results will improve.

3) Time Management

This is the third dimension of Zimmerman's model of SRL. Self-regulated learning requires organization and scheduling. Time management is basically just organization related to time. Because college profs don't give many reminders, you need to do a lot of planning on your own. To be good at this, you need planning skills and the ability to accurately estimate how much time you need to complete homework, assignments, and studying. You will read more about time and how to use it better in Key #7.

Self-regulated learning skills take time and practice to develop. SRL is all about planning, monitoring, and evaluating your efforts. It requires the use of metacognitive knowledge and skills. You should budget more time for studying to accommodate these more advanced thinking skills. This time "cost" is offset by all the benefits of developing a mastery goal orientation (see Key #3) and the higher level of achievement associated with metacognitive skills and self-regulated learning.[36] With practice, metacognitive skills and self-regulated learning make your studying more efficient.

4) Feedback

Receiving and learning from feedback is the fourth dimension of Zimmerman's model of SRL. Have you ever gotten an assignment or exam back and thought the comments were mean? Most teachers aren't mean, but they have very limited time. They don't have long to prepare you for your next class, never mind your career. They must communicate your strengths and weaknesses quickly. And don't forget: You are not the only one in the class. In college, profs are teaching hundreds of students each semester.

Teachers' and professors' comments should be considered, whether you like them or not. If you don't understand the feedback, *go ask.* Please keep in mind that compared to everything there is to know about a subject, you know very little. That's why you are in school. So, as hard as this is to believe, your paper/exam may not have been as good as you thought it was. Successful students see "failure" as an opportunity to learn, not as an attack on their character (remember Key #2, attributions). Successful students use the feedback to modify their strategies and efforts.

SUGGESTION #1: Understand that your success in school is about learning the material *and* learning what your teachers and professors expect and want. This varies from class to class. Research suggests that "students' success in college depends not only upon their explicit understanding of course content but also their implicit understanding of how to demonstrate that knowledge in ways that will satisfy each professor's expectations."[37] That means you must understand your teacher. Rather than guess at the expectations, *go ask.* Get feedback and more information about assignments, exams, and general expectations.

SUGGESTION #2: Look up the word "umbrageous." Get going. *Seriously.* You must look this one up. Please **go now**!

Did you find it? Did you find the part of the definition that applies to people? If that term applies to you, this is where you must begin. It is hard to learn from constructive criticism if you are umbrageous. Even if the teacher's feedback was not gentle, interpreting those comments as a personal attack will only make you ignore, dismiss, or argue against them. Please remember the importance of your attributions (Key #2). Consider the teacher's comments as suggestions about how to improve. This is important.

💡 **SUGGESTION #3:** This might sound nasty but, ***get over yourself***. As a student, you should expect to be imperfect. Getting 90-100% is (or should be) reserved for true excellence. It takes time, a lot of learning, a lot of screwing up, a lot of patience, and a lot of self-discipline to achieve excellence. Considering the feedback from someone who knows way more than you (e.g., your teacher or professor) is a good first step. Remember, you submit assignments and exams for evaluation. When you get the evaluation, regardless of whether it matches your expectations (Key #1), be grateful for the opportunity to learn from someone who is more educated and/or experienced. That perspective will serve you better than thinking the teacher/professor is a jerk.

SUGGESTION #4: Students with performance goals (Key #3) often only glance at the grade they receive and then discard the assignment.[38] However, especially for students who are somewhat uncertain about their abilities or who fear failure, feedback can point to strengths as well as offer useful suggestions about how to improve skills. This can help you feel more in control of your learning and grades.

In my experience, many students treat assignments like they are discrete, independent events that disappear (POOF!) once they are handed in. With that attitude, there would be no need to review the graded assignment and consider feedback. However, while any given assignment may be graded and done, there will be many more assignments that require you to use similar skills, such as understanding and following instructions, writing in a particular format, expressing complex relationships between topics, building an original idea, supporting and defending those ideas with research, comparing and contrasting a variety of viewpoints…the list goes on and on.

Feedback from teachers and professors can help you understand all of the above. Plus, as you get more feedback from different teachers and profs, you will have more and more perspectives about how to complete assignments effectively. Given that you are (or will be) paying for school, think of feedback as one of the important pieces of learning you are paying for.

5) The Environment

The environment is the fifth dimension of Zimmerman's model of SRL. No, he didn't mean global warming or clean energy. This refers to *where* you study. If your house is really noisy, is that an environment in which you want to study? Personally, I need silence to study well. But that's just me. The ultimate point is getting the results you want. If you are getting A's while studying in a construction zone or the middle of an amusement park, more power to you. If you are not getting A's, does your studying environment need modification? Finding a place free from distractions is usually helpful. Research has shown that students who deal more effectively with their studying environment are more likely to succeed, even compared to students who have an equal amount of academic ability.[39]

SUGGESTION #1: I always recommend a quiet place to study. That is my bias. Dorms can be crazy. If you have kids, well, they can be crazy, too (lol). Studying at work, where there are a lot of interruptions, can be tough. Sometimes students have to make do with what little time they have, so you may find yourself trying to study in these environments, and I respect your effort. But, whenever you have a choice, find a quiet place. Can you stay longer at school and use the library? If you are at home, will closing a door help? Can you walk to a quiet park or the lake and sit on a bench and read?

When I was in school, I stayed at the library until it closed. Then I would go to another building on campus and find an open classroom. I would stay there, alone, until I accomplished my (proximal) goals for the day.

I even used this suggestion when writing this book for you. I did some writing in a lawn chair on the shore of the lake near my home. At home, I keep things quiet. When I am at school, I close my office door. Yes, I take my own advice.

SUGGESTION #2: It is important to consider not just external distractions like noise, but internal distractions as well. Things like depression, anxiety, PTSD, relationship problems, drug and alcohol addiction, and bereavement don't just magically go away because it is time to study. They are *huge* internal distractions. Please do yourself an incredible kindness and find support and counseling. Talk to your doctor. Open up to your minister/pastor. Reach out to family members and friends. Do something to address these issues so they do not prevent you from achieving your goals. Most schools have resources and/or referral services. **Go ask**!

6) Other People

Dealing with other people is the sixth and final dimension of Zimmerman's model of SRL. "Wait, how is *self*-regulated learning about *others*? OK, Troy, you were making some sense until right now."

Please allow me to explain. Who you choose to study with is a very important decision (if you choose to work with others at all). Study groups can be very helpful. They can also be a disastrous waste of time. As well, you can choose certain professors, tutors, support staff, and friends as models and mentors. Choose carefully.

In school, some topics are confusing. Sometimes the instructions for assignments are not perfectly clear (much to the chagrin of the teacher who wrote them). For that matter, an entire course can be brutal. Actively seeking help from other people is an important part of SRL. Students who seek out their teachers, teaching assistants, and/or tutors are more likely to succeed than students who suffer in silence. Some students are afraid to ask questions and for help because they don't want to look stupid (remember Key # 1, 2, & 3). The only way you can be stupid is if you don't know *and* you don't ask (you will read about this more in Key #7).

SUGGESTION: An effective method of self-testing your knowledge is to evaluate others and be evaluated by others. This can work well when in a studying group. Here is a cool exercise: Have each member of the studying group write out some of the information you're studying but purposely make some errors. Then exchange papers and see if you can spot the mistakes. More importantly, can you correct the errors without looking things up? Finding and correcting errors is a great way to learn. Research has shown that students who participate in "peer assessment" activities get higher grades and have more positive attitudes toward learning. This kind of activity creates other benefits including more focused attention on the task and increased reflection on what is being studied (that is a metacognitive skill).[40]

In my opinion, this serves another very important function: It helps you deal effectively and in a non-threatening way with mistakes. Many students are afraid of mistakes. They react very defensively to comments that point out errors. Using mistakes in the manner described above can make them a powerful and non-threatening studying and learning tool.

Summary/General Suggestions

I know I said there were six parts in Zimmerman's model of SRL. Yes, I can count. The following list is a summary of information in two articles written by Zimmerman.[41,42] I thought you might use it as a type of checklist for your own behavior. If you see that you don't do some of these things, you can add them to your goals for a course. Pick just one thing and try to incorporate it into what you do this week. Making a little change now is the start of a good new habit, and reflects you have a growth mindset.

- Arrive prepared for and participate in class. Express interest in the subject.

- Offer relevant information and ideas that were not in the text when you participate.
- Express and defend opinions that differ from that of classmates and the teacher.
- Ask insightful questions.
- Volunteer for special/extra tasks or activities (if there is that opportunity).
- List what you want to accomplish when you study.
- Schedule studying and homework time every day.
- Complete assignments on time or early.
- Check work carefully (proofread) before turning it in.
- Keep track of completed assignments and what still needs to be completed.
- Seek help from the teacher if you're having difficulties.
- Solicit information from the teacher about upcoming tests/exams.
- Ask for additional details about teachers' expectations for assignments.
- Ask for more information about feedback you receive from the teacher.

Paul Pintrich's Model of SRL

Paul Pintrich was a leader in self-regulated learning. He suggested that SRL occurs in four phases and explained that, in these four phases, you must regulate your thoughts, motivation, feelings, behavior, and the environment.[43,44]

Phase 1 is ***forethought.*** This occurs *before* you start a task. For example, when you sit down to do a homework assignment, you can think about and plan what you need to do. You can think about the learning goals, what you already know about the topic, and meta-cognitive knowledge (your own achievement goal orientation, level of interest, level of self-efficacy, and thoughts about how easy or difficult things will be). You might also consider what extra materials you need, such as other books, notes, online resources, or even just a calculator.

Phase 2 is ***monitoring.*** This occurs *during* the task. Monitoring includes your level of attention to and awareness of what you are doing. That means metacognition (Key #6) plays a key role. During the monitoring phase, you think about how easy or hard the task is. You respond to metacognitive experiences such as the feeling of knowing or feeling of difficulty. These help you use metacognitive skills such as evaluating information and tracking progress toward your goal.[45] This helps you "discriminate between effective and ineffective performances."[46] Knowing when studying is effective, and when it is not, allows you to modify your efforts.

During this phase, you must also be aware of your motivation, feelings of efficacy (Key #4), and the attributions (Key #2) you make, especially if you are experiencing the feeling of difficulty (Key #5). Finally, monitoring includes practical issues such as time management and how much effort you are making.

Phase 3 is ***control.*** Again, this occurs *during* the task. You actively respond to the thoughts, feelings, and motivations you noticed and experienced during the monitoring phase. Control is exerted on your attention, effort, motivation, use of studying strategies, and aspects of the environment. You use studying strategies such as note-taking, re-reading, and memorizing. You use meta-cognitive skills such as positive self-talk. You structure your environment by turning off your phone. You may also seek help directly from a teacher, tutor, or classmate.[47]

Phase 4 is ***reaction and reflection***. This happens *after* the task has been completed. You consider how you believe you have done on the task. You think about your efforts. You make attributions about your performance. This phase can also include the attributions you make when you receive feedback from your instructor about how you did.

Within Pintrich's framework, we can see all the Psychological Keys to Student Success operating. Check this out:

- In the forethought phase, beliefs (Key #1) about learning and your goal orientation (Key #3) will affect your planning for the task you're working on.

- Confidence in your abilities (Key #4) is relevant to all three time frames (before, during, and after the task).

- During the task, metacognitive experiences (Key #5) help guide your effort and influence your attention and persistence.

- If you are having trouble during the task, you will generate explanations (Key #2) which will reflect your beliefs (Key #1) and locus of control (part of Key #2) which will, in turn, affect your motivation.

- After the task is done and you receive feedback (Key #6), you will again have to explain your grade (Key #2) and compare this outcome to your beliefs (Key #1), your confidence in your abilities (Key #4), and recognize any thinking errors (Key #7) you might have made.

FINAL THOUGHTS

My hope is that you are having "aha" moments. All the Psychological Keys are connected to each other and reflect **how you think**. If you want to succeed in school (and in life), this is where you must focus your efforts. **How you think** goes with you everywhere. You can't avoid it. So, do something about it.

Please consider this quotation: "It is not just the learner's cultural background, demographic characteristics, or personality that influence achievement and learning directly; nor are contextual characteristics of the classroom the only things that shape achievement; but it is the learner's self-regulation of his or her cognition, motivation, and behavior that mediates these relationships."[48] That quotation stresses that achievement is a complex interaction of many variables, but explaining how you do in school is primarily about your own thinking, motivation, and behavior.

Now that you are totally convinced that **how you think** is the key to your success, let's consider some common thinking errors. Understanding thinking errors and how to avoid them is Key #7.

KEY #7 – AVOIDING THINKING ERRORS

Overestimating your abilities and knowledge can lead you to underestimate your learning and studying needs. This is perhaps the biggest mistake of all.

A lot of the information we have covered so far requires you to develop self-awareness. Confucius, the Chinese philosopher who lived over 500 years before Christ, suggested that real knowledge is about knowing the extent of your own ignorance. LOL. That's encouraging. So, you're smart when you realize that you don't know much? Yes, that's the idea.

The seventh Psychological Key to Student Success is about understanding common thinking errors that people make. By knowing these common errors, you can take steps to reduce them and become a more successful student.

Psychological research shows a disturbing trend: We believe that we know more than we do. Here are a few examples:

- Teenage boys rated their knowledge about how to use condoms as much higher than their actual knowledge of condom use.[1]

- Surgical residents' ratings of their surgical skills did not match their performance on standard board exams of surgical knowledge.[2]

- Students who lack reading skills fail to know when they have accurately understood a reading.[3]

- College students who reported feeling 100% confidence in their answers were only 80% correct.[4]

These examples make clear the importance of accurately assessing your own knowledge and skills. Overestimating your abilities can lead you to underestimate your studying and learning needs. For example, overconfidence in what you know can lead you to not plan enough studying time. The result can be studying less and, therefore, achieving at a lower level than you expected.

Anyone, regardless of skill level, can overestimate how good he/she is at being a student. Becoming more self-aware and improving metacognitive skills (Key #5) are important because, "to the degree that people judge themselves accurately, they make decisions, big and small that lead to better lives."[5]

The Dunning-Kruger Effect

Justin Kruger and David Dunning stated that "when people are incompetent in the strategies they adopt to achieve success and satisfaction, they suffer a dual burden: Not only do they reach erroneous conclusions and make unfortunate choices, but their incompetence robs them of the ability to realize it."[6] Basically this means that when you don't know something, you make mistakes and don't realize you are making the mistakes.

Let me give you a personal example. There is a cool word that describes when we feel mentally weary, a little like when we are bored and under-stimulated. The word is "ennui." When I first started using the word, I had no idea I was pronouncing it incorrectly. I didn't know so I didn't recognize that there was a problem and I kept making the mistake. No one ever corrected me. It was only when I heard someone say it properly (it is pronounced *on-wee*) that I clued in to my mistake.

Fortunately, I learned from my mistake. However, sometimes when people are corrected, they have trouble believing the feedback so they don't learn from their poor performance.[7] When people believe their error is in fact correct, they may actually believe that those who have the right answer are wrong.[8] The point is, *it is hard to learn when you think you don't have anything to learn*! Add to this another interesting research finding – the more times we recall information, the more confident we are that it is correct, even if the information we recall repeatedly is wrong.[9]

The Dunning-Kruger Effect in School

Dunning and Kruger suggested the skills that make us good at something are the same skills we need to evaluate if we (or others) are, in fact, good at it. Therefore, if you lack effective studying skills, it will be difficult to effectively evaluate your studying skills. Back in the day, we used to call this a "double whammy."

As you might imagine, this effect can significantly impact your ability to predict exam performance. A 2001 research study found that first-year students' beliefs (Key #1) about their academic skills did not match well with the evaluations they received from their instructors.[10] A survey completed in the 1970s showed that 70 percent of high school seniors estimated they had "above average" leadership abilities.[11] How can 70 percent of students be in the top 50 percent (average) of anything? That is statistically impossible! The mismatch between beliefs about our own skills and how we are evaluated is common and occurs in many professions, not just with students. For these reasons I strongly encourage students to talk to their teachers and professors. You need to learn how successful students study, read, write, and take notes. Assume nothing.

Remember the study I mentioned in Key #1 regarding students' beliefs about strategies for studying for tests? I cited a study in which only 11 percent of undergraduates practiced recalling information (i.e., self-testing) in preparation for a test, suggesting that 89 percent did not know about the benefits of self-testing.[12] If you don't know about a strategy, you don't use it and don't realize that you're making a mistake by not using it. That's the Dunning-Kruger effect. This is one reason why learning a variety of studying skills is important.

Speaking of double whammies – it turns out the lowest-performing students are the most likely to overestimate how they are doing in a course. In one study, researchers had 141 psychology students estimate how they had just done on an exam. Students who performed the worst were the students who most overestimated their performance. They overestimated their performance by approximately 30 percent.[13] That is the equivalent of three letter grades. A 2006 study showed that weaker students were the most optimistic, but least accurate, in predicting how they were doing in a course.[14] In another study, when students were asked to predict which questions they got right and wrong on an exam, weaker students were less able to accurately predict exactly what they got correct and incorrect.[15]

Unfortunately, this tendency to grossly overestimate performance persists for these weaker students even in the face of continuous negative feedback on exams.[16] The key to breaking this pattern is to recognize it and do something about it. If you are getting poor grades in a class, make sure you ask teachers and professors about why you're doing poorly. Ask for more explanation of difficult concepts. Seek tutoring in subjects that are challenging for you. Learn more and better studying skills. Take action!

Overestimating your ability can also undermine your motivation to learn. When it comes to self-regulated learning (Key #6), why would you bother to work harder if you don't think you have anything to learn?[17] Why would you bother to consider feedback from your teachers or professors if you believe you are more skilled than you are? The monitoring and evaluating that is essential to SRL will be reduced by such ignorance.

SUGGESTION #1: Do not feel bad. Everyone is ignorant (by the way, ignorance simply means you don't know something). Compared to what we know, there is a ton of information out there we don't know. Walk into any library and look at all those books. How much of that do you think you know?!?!

SUGGESTION #2: Even when you feel like you know something really well, always assume that there is much more to it that you don't know. If you are completely certain of your knowledge, realize that there are connections between what you know and other things you don't. So, there's always more to learn. Stay curious. (Also look back at the chart in Key #1...thinking that you know it all is very naïve.)

Here is an example. Pretend that you are studying physics and learn Newton's third law. This law states that every action has an equal and opposite reaction. You read about this and understand all the examples in your physics text and from the lectures by your professor. On the exam, you get the questions correct. So, you know it, right? Maybe you really do. But think about this: The next time you yell at someone and that person stops talking to you, could that be an example of Newton's third law? Maybe not talking to you is an "equal and opposite reaction" to you yelling? If we just think in terms of physics, that relationship example would never come to mind. You see, there are always new and different perspectives to learn. (Comparing physics and relationships is a great metaphor – remember what I said about metaphors in the first suggestion for the interest section in Key #3?)

SUGGESTION #3: Take a lesson from skilled professionals and experts. Compared to students and people with less knowledge and experience, skilled professionals and experts ask more relevant questions, request more information, and look for new information rather than assume they fully understand a problem or project.[18] If asking questions and double-checking that they're on the right track works for professionals and experts, perhaps it will work for you.

Errors of Omission

When trying to solve a problem, we are only aware of possible solutions that we can bring to mind. Obviously, we can't think of the possible solutions we haven't thought of. That's the idea behind errors of omission. The solution we come up with is great if it works, but there might be a lot of other solutions we didn't come up with.

Why does this matter? Here is a research example. When people were asked to estimate how they did solving a Boggle puzzle (making words out of a 4x4 grid of random letters), they rated their performance based on how many words they found, not how many words they might have missed. People did poorly when they were asked to judge how many words they missed.[19]

Another good example comes from research that asked participants to find as many words as they could in the letters that make up the word "spontaneous." How do you think you would do? Let's say you come up with 100 words. That sounds good, right? Well, there are more than 1,300 English words that can be made from those letters.[20] This demonstrates that we overestimate what we know, how this overestimation leads to false feelings of confidence in our abilities, and how much we miss and really don't know.

In school, you might think that a grade of 80% on a test is pretty good. But what information was in the 20 percent you missed? Do you want your surgeon missing 20 percent? How about your lawyer, accountant, or the contractor building your house?

There is good news that comes from this idea about errors of omission. When you make people aware of their errors of omission, they become more accurate in self-assessing their own performance.[21] For students, this is a crucial element of learning. Seeking out and paying close attention to feedback from teachers can greatly enhance not just your actual knowledge, but also your awareness of the things you didn't consider. This is very true of studying skills as well. You can't use more effective studying strategies if you don't know they exist.

This book is designed to give you a lot of information and feedback about things you didn't know and didn't consider so that you can stop making a lot of psychological errors of omission!!

Tendency to "Self-enhance"

Some things in school (and in life) are clear-cut. Two plus two equals four. Water makes you wet (and sustains your life). But, in many other cases, the "right" answer is not so straightforward. This is true in psychology pretty much all the time. Dealing with thoughts, feelings, and behaviors can be very complex; there are many perspectives and potentially correct answers.

Research has found that when situations and personal characteristics are unclear, we tend to "self-enhance."[22] For example, people are more likely to rate themselves as higher than average on a personal quality like "being considerate" (that can be interpreted many ways) than on a quality that is easier to measure, such as punctuality.

In psychology, there are three common examples of our tendency to self-enhance. The **self-serving bias** occurs when you attribute (Key #2) your own successes to personal qualities like intelligence but attribute your failures to external factors such as an unfair situation. As well, research shows that if we are skilled in some area (e.g., math, writing, fixing the car, etc.), we tend to believe that area is more strongly related to intelligence than areas where we lack skill.[23]

Confirmation bias occurs when you look for information that "proves" your belief to be correct. Face it, we like to be right, especially when dealing with our deeply held beliefs. If you believe that you are smart, you will look for "evidence" that you are smart. You will point out and remember things you did that are "smart." If you believe that someone is mean, you will look for and point out "evidence" that the person is mean. This tendency to try and prove ourselves right partially explains why we sometimes cling strongly to ideas that are not entirely accurate. For example, some students believe they are great students in college because they got A's in high school, even though they are getting C's and D's in college right now.

Sometimes our assessment of our abilities is inaccurate because we *fail to consider the ability of others*. Pretend that someone asks you: Compared to other students, how good you are at finding your way around campus? Chances are, and research has shown, that you will probably rate yourself as above average. You make this rating on the basis that you have no problem getting around campus, totally ignoring the fact that most other students also have no problem getting around campus.[24] Similarly, if I asked you to judge your ability to get an A in an advanced astrophysics course, you'd likely rate your ability as lower than others, missing the fact that many other students are also not likely to be very good at astrophysics.

Hindsight

Have you ever struggled with a math problem and, before you finished it, looked up the answer in the back of the book? When you saw the answer, did you suddenly feel like the answer was obvious? "Oh. I knew that!" Well, I have a tough question for you: If you knew it, why couldn't you figure it out without looking?

Have you ever been reviewing an exam you got back, where the correct answers are provided for items you got wrong and exclaimed, "I knew that! Why did I pick that other answer?" Well, I know why. You did *not* know the answer, no matter what you say about it *after* the fact. If you knew it, you would have gotten it right the first time. This tendency to say we knew the right answer after it is given to us is called the hindsight bias.

SUGGESTION: When you are working on a problem or when you are struggling to remember a detail you studied, looking up the answer and recognizing it is *not* the same as remembering it. The important question you should be asking is why you didn't remember the information without looking it up. This is a key meta-cognitive skill. Only when you can correctly recall information *repeatedly without help* and *after a delay* has true learning occurred. So, beware of the hindsight bias. Always test yourself. Test yourself repeatedly over many days on everything you are studying, even if you feel you already know it.

Time

There is a tendency for us to underestimate how much time we need to complete a task, in part because we also tend to overestimate our ability to get things done. This is called **planning fallacy**. We focus too narrowly on the task at hand and ignore or discount the probability of other reasonably predictable events getting in the way.[25] This is especially relevant to today's college student who has a host of other obligations (i.e., jobs, kids, family, commuting, etc.) competing for a fixed amount of time.

Research has suggested that people should focus more attention on the possible circumstances that may arise and plan accordingly.[26] Planning that is based simply on "I have five math problems that should take a half hour" is a very perfect-world scenario based on no interruptions and no difficulties. Unfortunately, we don't live in a perfect world. That means an old saying is good advice: Plan for the worst and hope for the best. It is better to plan more time and have time leftover if you finish early than it is to plan a set amount of time and run out before you get things done. Part of the problem occurs when you write "do assignment" or "study for exam" in your schedule. Those scheduled activities give no indication of how much there is to know or how hard that information will be to learn.

SUGGESTION #1: A great strategy to keep yourself in tune with what you need to study for exams is to make a list of terms, names, dates, textbook pages covered, theories, etc. at the end of every class session. If you do this every day you will quickly see how much you cover in a class before each exam and, therefore, how much time it will likely take to learn *all* that information. Reviewing like this at the end of each class will also help you think about and remember the information in the first place.

The "discrepancy-reduction model"[27] attempts to explain why and how students use their studying time. It suggests that you first try to figure out what you need to do and how you will do it. Once that is sorted out, you will choose a studying strategy for the material that must be studied. Finally, you will monitor (Keys #5 & 6) how well you are learning the material. If the material has been learned, then studying can be reduced or stopped. If not, more studying needs to be done.

Does this seem like what you do? Well, it depends on what your studying goals are. If you are out of time, you won't be able to study more. If you are running out of time, you might choose to reinforce your understanding of the easy material. However, when the goal is mastery, you are more likely to study the material you judge as difficult first and longer.[28]

Your choice of what to study is not guided only by how hard you think the material is. There are many factors that influence your studying. One is how much time you have. Lisa Son and Janet Metcalfe did three experiments and found that when students feel they are under a lot of time pressure, they are more likely to focus their studying time on material they judge as easier.[29] The implication is clear: If you don't have much time, you are more likely to study the easiest material before an exam; but if the difficult material is on the exam, you have a serious problem. This stresses the importance of developing stronger time management skills so you have enough time to study everything thoroughly.

SUGGESTION #2: A study done in 2002 examined students' confidence in their ability to accomplish a task. First, students were asked to estimate how much time they thought they would need to do a task in order to feel 50 percent sure they'd get it done in time. Then, they were asked to estimate how much (more) time they thought they would need to complete the same task so they felt 99 percent sure they'd get it done in time. You would think that the 99 percent rating would be a pretty good estimate and that most would get the task done in time. Nope. Only 45 percent of them got the task done in time despite being 99 percent sure they would be able to do so.[30]

Given that college is supposed to be a challenging experience, designed to prepare you for harder classes and eventually a career, you should expect to encounter difficult material on exams. You must make sure you have enough time to study. If you have many other responsibilities, this will be hard. We all have the same 24/7 to work with. You must plan ahead and start studying many days, even weeks before an exam in order to learn difficult material. As an example of this, many college professors feel that students should spend two hours studying outside of class for every hour spent in class. That is good information for you to know when you plan what classes to take and how much time you should devote to studying.

SUGGESTION #3: I advise students to adopt a simple weekly strategy. On Sunday night, look at your schedule for the coming week. You see what you have planned. Now try to anticipate likely delays and the needs of other people. Check the weather. Are there birthdays? Is someone ill? No one expects you to be able to predict everything, but you can think ahead and build in some time buffers for your most important obligations and task deadlines.

A time management problem occurs "when people concentrate [on what they have to do] and ignore the knowable fact that background circumstances from everyday life often sneak in to interfere with one's plans."[31] That means we can get so focused on what we need to get done, we fail to anticipate problems that could arise. When developing software, Microsoft builds in an extra 30 percent more time to the development schedule over and above the estimated project completion time.[32] If that kind of planning strategy is good enough for one of the most successful companies in the world, it should be good enough for you to at least try. Build in more time than you think you need.

Honest Feedback

When you get an assignment or exam back, read the comments and consider them carefully. If the comments are hard to understand or are unclear, go and talk to the teacher or professor.

Most importantly, if there are few or no comments to help explain your (good or bad) grade, you must go ask. A particularly important opportunity to learn is lost when you don't know what you did wrong and what you could do to improve.

SUGGESTION #1: Remember that the Dunning-Kruger effect states when we lack skill we are more likely to make mistakes and not realize it. The best way to address it is to get honest feedback about what you are doing wrong, where your skills are weak or lacking, and what you can improve. Remember errors of omission? To avoid them, ask instructors specifically what you may have missed or what you could have added that you didn't think of. Ask them what they would add to (or remove from) your assignment if they were doing it, not just grading it. And here is an interesting connection with Key #1: When you ask for feedback, make sure you ask for advice on strategies, effort, and other things you can control. Such feedback can help you develop a growth mindset.[33]

SUGGESTION #2: Even when you ask, sometimes the feedback you get from your instructors just isn't detailed enough to be helpful.[34] Teachers are human and, like you, are very busy. As well, some teachers are afraid to hurt other people's feelings. Many are uncomfortable with criticism, conflict, and confrontation in their personal lives, so they avoid these things at all costs. If your instructors have these fears, they may not tell you the whole truth when they give feedback. You might think, "Ya, but teachers are supposed to be professionals who should tell me the truth." You are right. They should. But many believe that negative feedback will hurt your self-esteem. Research shows, however, it is more important that you get accurate feedback about what you can and cannot do.[35]

SUGGESTION #3: Don't let this happen. Go and ask your instructors specifically for honest and more detailed feedback. When you talk to them, express that it is important to your learning that you get the whole, unadulterated truth. Let them know you can handle some constructive criticism because the rockin', long-haired psychology prof who wrote this awesome book said it was OK.

Holly Hassel and Jessica Lourey noted that instructors are also afraid of negative evaluations from students. The reason is that those evaluations can impact instructors' job security (sad but sometimes true). So, instructors try to keep students happy. That means they might inflate your grade and might not tell you the whole truth about your performance.[36] This, unfortunately, is a problem in the college system that can get in your way. Ask profs to explain what you did well and what you did poorly so you understand your strengths, weaknesses, and learning needs.

Choice

Normally, having choices is a good thing. However, making choices can sometimes lead to a thinking error. There is something called the "illusion of control." It says that people will sometimes believe they control chance events.[37] How does this relate to you and school? Well, you choose your classes. You choose to attend classes and participate. You become familiar with the material by simply showing up. These choices and sense of familiarity can make you think you know the material better than you do. Your choices and familiarity do not guarantee that you have skills related to those classes. To avoid the illusion of control, please make sure you study often, thoroughly, and well.

FINAL THOUGHTS

Your effort and persistence have guided you through the seven Psychological Keys to Student Success. The learning you are doing will serve you well in school and in your life. With all your new knowledge, and the thinking skills you are developing, it is time to consider how the Keys can be understood differently depending on culture.

CULTURE – THE THINKING SKILLS KEYCHAIN

We must respect the rich diversity that exists in perspectives, experiences, learning styles, and motivation when considering what it means to be a successful student (and person).

In a classic research study, American and Japanese university students were shown animated scenes of fish swimming. The fish were in the foreground and were more prominent than the plants and smaller creatures in the background. When asked to remember what they saw, Japanese students recalled more of the smaller creatures in the background and explained the relationships between items in the scene. In contrast, American students remembered details about the big fish in the foreground.[1]

Up to this point, most of what we have considered has been based on Western theories, beliefs, values, and research. "Western models of achievement motivation have at times been criticized as being culturally entrenched in an ideology of individualism."[2] That means a lot of research on academic achievement has a Western bias. But now more than ever, students at all levels of education

---

are a richly diverse group. Within that diversity are students with markedly different upbringings, heritages, and customs as well as socioeconomic status and whether they are first-, second-, or later-generation students.[3]

So, in order to really appreciate the Psychological Keys to Student Success, you have to understand that the seven Keys are held together on a special keychain. That keychain is your culture. "Culture is the behaviors, ideas, attitudes, values and traditions shared by a group of people and transmitted from one generation to the next."[4] All the things that make up your culture have shaped how you approach school and learning.[5] Culture influences how you perceive people and situations, how you organize your thoughts and knowledge,[6] and how you define things like achievement, effort, success, and failure.[7]

At some point during your education, you will probably encounter a comparison between "individualistic" and "collectivist" cultures. Individualistic cultures tend to emphasize the uniqueness of the individual, personal fulfillment individual achievement, and feeling good about oneself. In contrast, collectivist cultures tend to emphasize the importance of the family, how each person can contribute to the betterment of the group, and how achievement includes that sense of obligation to the group and family. Said another way, individualistic cultures value independence; collectivist cultures value interdependence.

There are many ways people from individualistic and collectivist cultures differ. However, I am *not* telling you that *all* people from individualistic cultures are the same. Likewise, I am *not* telling you that *all* people from collectivist cultures are the same. I'm simply pointing out patterns that have been observed and researched across many different fields of study. As the old saying goes, it would be very wrong to paint everyone with the same brush.

Understanding that I am ***not*** stereotyping diverse groups of people, here are some examples of reliable differences observed when comparing individualistic and collectivist cultures on topics you have learned about so far. These are offered to illustrate the importance of culture when considering the Psychological Keys to Student Success.

1. Motivation in individualistic cultures often comes from "actions that allow expression of one's important self-defining, inner attributes" compared to in collectivist cultures where people are more motivated by "actions that enhance or foster one's relatedness or connection to others."[8]

2. Getting involved in your campus and college community has been shown to increase achievement and persistence, especially among minority students.[9] In one study of 16 African American college undergraduates, the students felt empowered by knowledge and the feeling it could serve their community. Education was viewed as a path to better circumstances. Developing critical thinking and speaking up during class discussions about ethnicity and race were seen as important aspects of academic success.[10]

3. Research has shown that people from collectivist cultures are more likely to make external attributions for success and make internal attributions for failures. That is, they may give credit to the group for success but assume personal responsibility for failures. This pattern, one different from the common Western pattern, motivates them for future tasks.[11]

4. The motivation you have for educational and career goals are also influenced by cultural upbringing. In individualist cultures, goals are often set for individual achievement. In collectivist cultures, personal goals

commonly reflect a desire to help others to meet their goals; personal and group goals are related.[12] As well, compared to students from individualistic cultures, students from collectivist cultures such as Japan have been shown to experience higher academic achievement when motivated by the fear of failure.[13]

5. Culture influences your beliefs in your abilities. For ethnically diverse first-generation students, self-efficacy is a reliable predictor of academic performance, GPA, and staying in school.[14] This is important because first-generation students face more challenges (e.g., need to work, fewer hours available to study, lower preparation for college) than traditional students. In addition, first-generation Hispanic students may more frequently be torn between traditional family responsibilities and their individual academic obligations and needs.[15]

6. How you respond to feedback is an aspect of self-regulated learning that varies depending on culture. For example, people from collectivist cultures often view criticism and negative feedback as more accurate, credible, and helpful than praise. That lies in stark contrast to our desire to promote and preserve high self-esteem in individualistic cultures.

7. Culture also influences how you define what it means to be intelligent. In individualistic cultures (such as those in the United States, Canada, Western Europe, and Australia), intelligence is something that resides inside the individual; "whether the right stuff is DNA, genes, neurons, hormones, traits, abilities, motivation, drive, or talent, it is what is inside that counts."[16]

However, other cultures around the world view intelligence differently:

a. Japanese culture values sociability, leadership, sympathy, social modesty, and having control over one's inner state as aspects of intelligent thought;

b. Indian culture values the connection between intelligence and morality and respect for elders, parents, and guests;

c. Chinese culture values the social and hierarchical nature of knowledge and respects those who are more knowledgeable;

d. Ugandan culture values intelligence as slow, deliberate, and helpful to others;

e. Puerto Rican culture values harmony within the group, as well as respect, obedience, and conformity.[17]

As you can see, culture is the context in which you grow and develop your most important beliefs and ideas. These become the bedrock for your approach to education. The Psychological Keys to Student Success are all on your cultural keychain.

FINAL THOUGHTS

In my experience teaching students from many cultural backgrounds, the desire to do well in school and create better lives for themselves and their families is a huge driving factor. I'm inspired every day by the resilience, dedication, and effort of the students I teach. Sometimes I even feel a little guilty – I get paid to be the teacher but I often feel that I learn more from you than you learn from me!

There are many dimensions of culture on which people differ. This brief section has highlighted only one such dimension – individualism and collectivism. Religion, family and gender roles, geographic location, and socio-economic status are examples of other very influential factors you could consider as part of culture. Please know I understand there is much more to the story and I respect the complexity and richness of cultural differences, as I hope you do too.

With greater appreciation for the power of **how you think**, now you are ready to learn **how to learn**. It is finally the right time to think about studying skills. I am about to share some powerful learning strategies that will make another big difference in **how you think**!

SECTION 3:
LEARNING SKILLS

POWERFUL LEARNING STRATEGIES

*Learning requires a lot more than studying. Successful students use a greater variety of strategies and they use them more frequently than less successful students. You are about to **learn how to learn** and totally rock your assignments and exams.*

Elementary and high school teachers go to college and get a degree in Education. They learn about how kids and teenagers grow and develop. This helps them understand what youth of different ages can and cannot do and understand. Teachers learn about different teaching methods and different learning styles. They learn how to create lesson plans and curriculum. Basically, they learn how to teach.

College professors also go to college. Almost all of them go to college for a long time and get graduate degrees in a certain specialty. Most college professors have a "doctorate" (a PhD). Others, like me, have a Master's degree (that is not as much education as a PhD, but

I'm still cool). Overall, college professors have a lot of education in their area of specialty.

Guess what. Most university professors never learn anything about how to teach. They don't get a degree in Education, so they aren't taught how to teach other people. Universities hire them because they are experts in their field, not because they know how to teach. There is considerably more focus on teaching at the community college level but, again, the average community college instructor does not have a degree in Education.

Why am I telling you this? I wrote this book so that you can help yourself. In college, you will have some fantastic professors. You are also going to have some professors who have no clue how to teach. In this section of the book, you will learn information, research, strategies, and techniques from Educational Psychology. This is the stuff elementary and high school teachers learn about. Basically, I'm giving you insider information about how to teach. If you understand this stuff, you can teach yourself how to learn. Are you following me? I'm trying to turn you into your own teacher for the times when your teachers and professors suck. LOL

As you now understand, I believe students must be taught how to learn, and that teachers should tell students specifically how to study.[1] My goal is to help you "create and understand the meaning" of what you are trying to learn.[2] Most college professors are not experts in teaching. When they tell you about studying strategies, it does not guarantee that the strategies are the most effective.

There are many common studying strategies such as reading, re-reading, highlighting, memorizing, summarizing, note-taking, and using flash cards. Many students use these. I hate to be the bearer of bad news but these are the weakest, least efficient strategies you can use.[3] Here is some more bad news. There are many studying strategies books out there. The majority are long, too general, and are not based on actual research.[4]

Now let me give you good news. There are many learning strategies that are very effective. The most successful students use a greater variety of learning strategies, and they use them more frequently, compared to less successful students.[5] In this section you will learn strategies that will help you remember, understand, and apply what you study far better than the usual list of studying strategies. The learning strategies will also help you utilize metacognition and become a successful self-regulated learner.[6] The ideas are powerful tools you can add to your learning toolkit.

Chunking

Let's get started with a fundamental and well-researched aspect of human memory. George Miller famously used the phrase "the magical number seven" to describe your short-term memory's capacity. Short-term memory temporarily holds information in your mind as you try to turn it into a more permanent, long-term memory. It is a crucial part of how we learn but it has a space limitation. Your short-term memory is able to hold 7 pieces of information, plus or minus two. That means you can only hold five to nine individual pieces of information in your short-term memory at a time.[7]

Have you ever noticed how many times you have to look up as you copy notes from the board or screen? How many words can you write down before you have to look up again? My bet is on five to nine words! That is a practical, classroom example of your short-term memory at work. Now imagine the times when you are reading a chapter in the textbook. How much information do you honestly think you can pack into your short-term memory as you try to encode it into long-term memories?

There is a helpful trick to expand the capacity of your short-term memory. George Miller called it "chunking."[8] Chunking involves taking individual pieces of information (like numbers, letters, or words) and combining them so there aren't as many individual pieces to remember. Here is another metaphor: think about shopping bags. At the grocery store, after you pay, you do not carry each individual grocery item to the car, one by one. You combine your purchases into bags so they are easier to carry. This is, in effect, how chunking helps your memory. It combines things so they are easier to carry (remember).

One of the best examples of this is a ten-digit phone number. Ten digits is bigger than the capacity of short-term memory. But look at those wonderful dashes separating the numbers!

123-456-7890

In that example, you can see how ten numbers actually become a chunk of three (area code), another chunk of three (called the prefix), and a chunk of four (called the line number). By combining the individual digits into chunks like this, you reduce the number of things to remember from ten to three.

Here is a question I ask students all the time: Would you rather read a book with four, 25-page chapters, or a book with twenty-five, 4-page chapters? Many students prefer the idea of more but shorter chapters. Why? Shorter chapters are more manageable. It is easier to keep track of the details. It is easier to stay focused. And, you feel as if you are making more progress as you complete one chapter after the next. Gone is the urge to flip forward and count how many pages are left (you know you do it) because the "end" of the chapter is always in sight.

SUGGESTION: Read the detailed table of contents for a chapter before you try to read the chapter.

It will show you how the chapter is divided into sections. The sections, prepared for you by the authors, are your chunks. This will help you to organize your thinking and studying. Read one section. Take a short break. Come back and read the next section. Do this for the whole chapter.

You can also apply this idea to organizing your class notes. By using headings, you break up all the words into chunks of related ideas. Not only does this help you organize your notes, it will help you think about and remember the information when it is time to study.

Self-testing

This is the biggest, best, greatest, most awesome learning strategy of them all. It is called self-testing. Simply put, "the act of taking an initial test improves performance on a later test."[9]

Good teachers know that active learning is more effective than passive learning in the classroom; the same is true when you are studying. Rather than passively reviewing your books and re-reading notes, put them away and, instead, try to actively recall the information you have been studying.

Here is what I tell my students to do. As you study, write down the basic terms, concepts, names, and theories on a separate sheet of paper. Write these down but just the names – no details. When you have finished reviewing a chapter or your notes, put your books and notes away, take a short break, and then try to fill out all the details for each term, concept, name, and theory from memory. No peeking.

When you do this, you are basically making a fill-in-the-blanks test for yourself; the blanks are just big. Using these open-ended questions is better than multiple-choice practice tests often given by your profs, but all types of self-testing are better than no self-testing at all.[10,11] Using fill-in-the-blanks or short-answer self-testing questions also makes the self-test more challenging, which has been shown to be better for your memory, even if it seems hard at first.[12] The benefits of self-testing are even greater when you take a break between studying and self-testing. It is more of a workout for your long-term memory and that improves learning.[13]

Self-testing requires you to think about what you know. It requires you to be aware of how easily you may recall some information and how difficult it is for you to remember other information. Testing yourself while studying also requires you to monitor your concentration and learning as you study. It makes you think about your thinking, engage in self-monitoring and self-control, and provide yourself with feedback. I have already told you about the power of metacognition. Self-testing is a learning strategy has been shown to improve metacognition.[14]

In a 2013 article, John Dunlosky pointed out many benefits of self-testing. First, correctly recalling information from memory helps you form long-term memories for that information. Second, if you make mistakes or cannot recall information during self-testing (that's the metacognitive feeling of difficulty), this helps you know to study that information more. You should continue studying until you can recall each term, concept, and theory at least once.[15]

Despite its effectiveness, students do not usually use self-testing, and they tend to persist in using less effective methods such as re-reading and highlighting.[16] This is less tiring and effortful, but it is also much less effective. It is too bad students choose to waste time with weak strategies when there are better ways.

Some professors test students at the end of a lecture to see what the students learned during the lecture. This might seem a little bit mean at first, but there is method to the madness. Testing students on the most important ideas at the end of the lecture can help them remember the most important material later. A research study showed that students who were tested like this did better on exams. Comments from the students themselves indicated that they felt they could "identify important topics, monitor their learning, increase their attendance, and pay more attention to lectures."[17] Research shows that questions like these help you honestly assess your knowledge and devote more time to studying what you need to.[18] This kind of testing after a lecture can increase critical thinking skills and decrease test-anxiety.[19] This relates to Key #7 and making sure you are not fooling yourself about what you know.

The point I want to stress is that even if your teachers and professors don't use this kind of testing, you can do it for yourself right after class. Take a few minutes to, from memory, write down some of the key ideas from the lecture. Then compare this with your notes to make certain you are on track. Many teachers and professors don't know about this nifty, simple, and efficient strategy, but now you do.

Successive Relearning & Spaced Review

When you use self-testing, it is not enough to remember something correctly only once. Don't get me wrong. That is good, but it is just a start. You will learn more if you remember something correctly over and over, so test yourself repeatedly over time.[20]

Successive relearning "involves self-testing until you can correctly recall the target information from memory and, [most importantly], doing so in more than one practice session."[21] To use this powerful learning strategy successfully, you must do some other things too:

1. You must plan to study the information repeatedly over many days. That means you must plan daily study sessions. No cramming!

2. You must study the information and then self-test during every study session.

3. Each time you self-test, you need to look up the answers, after you have tried to remember the information, to make sure you are getting everything correct.

4. During a single study session, you can stop testing on a concept once you recall it correctly, but self-test all concepts again the next time you study.

5. Pay attention to information you repeatedly have trouble learning.[22]

As you can see, this strategy requires time. You must plan to study every day for many days if you want this to work. Spreading studying out like that is called "spaced review." I wish I could tell you a strategy that will make learning fast and easy, but that is not how learning usually works. If you want to do well in college, self-testing, successive relearning, and spaced review are gold. Research has shown that using these strategies can improve your scores an entire letter grade and increase your ability to remember information for a long time.[23]

Flashcards – Making Them Useful

Students often talk about using flashcards as a studying strategy. However, many seem puzzled when I ask, "Ya, but do you actually know how to use them?" Let's consider the basic strategy and then we can understand the problems with flashcards and how to fix them.

With flashcards, you need to buy or make small cards. For all the concepts you think are important in a chapter or set of lecture notes, you write the term, theory name, person's name, or the concept on one side of the card and then you write details on the other side of the card. For example, if you were studying for a psychology exam on behaviorism, you might write "John Watson" on one side of a card and "Little Albert experiment," "classical conditioning," and "tabula rasa" on the other side.

John Watson	Little Albert experiment Classical conditioning "Tabula rasa" (blank slate)

You might be wondering, "Troy, you said there are problems with this strategy. What are they?"

I'm glad you asked because you know I'm going to tell you. The most obvious problem is that this strategy will take a lot of time. If you're studying for an exam that covers four chapters, there will be a ton of terms, names, theories, and concepts for which you must make flashcards. But, there are much bigger problems.

Students don't realize how time-consuming making flashcards is, which leaves them less time to review the cards once they are made. Making the cards is a huge time vampire. But, once the stack of flashcards is made, two more problems arise. First, many students only study what they put on the flashcards. They think they can simply put their books and notes away. However, there is no guarantee that they have written all the important, relevant material that needs to be studied onto the flashcards.

Second, and more problematic, is that students don't know how to use the cards once they are made. They read the term on one side, quickly flip the card over, and read the details on the other. Then they go to the next card, proceeding this way through the entire stack. Students go through the stack a few times and think that they are studying. Here's a question: How is this any different than just reviewing your notes? Yes, I realize you wrote things out, but now you are just reading and re-reading. You could have done that without the cards. Whether you re-read your notes or re-read the information on cards makes no difference. This is a passive strategy that requires very little thought.[24]

Yet another problem is that students "drop" cards from the stack they are studying once they feel like they know the information. Sometimes, cards are skipped simply because time is running out. Even worse is that students just want to "get it over with" and stop studying.[25]

Here is the key. Are you ready? The purpose of flashcards is *self-testing*. You are supposed to read the term on one side and then try to recall the details on the other side without looking. For flashcards to be useful, you must treat them like quiz questions. Try to remember all the details before you flip the card over. When you do flip the card over, evaluate how much you knew. You must go through the cards this way until you know everything you wrote down. Yes, everything. And remember what you just learned about successive relearning and spaced review. You must test yourself on everything over and over.

That's it. That is what you need to know about flashcards. If you have time to make them, knock yourself out. Just make sure that you use them properly.

SUGGESTION: Personally, I recommend that you "over-study" and demonstrate to yourself that you can correctly recall all the information repeatedly, especially after a delay of hours and even days. That fits with what you've already learned about self-testing, successive relearning, and spaced review.

Bloom's Taxonomy

There are many kinds of exam questions – multiple choice, fill-in-the-blanks, matching, short answer, essays, etc. However, have you ever noticed that some exam questions are easy, and others are very hard? Have you ever wondered why? I am going to tell you about something from Educational Psychology that, unless you are a Psychology or Education major, you probably would never hear about. It is going to make your studying a ton more effective.

One reason exam questions may seem difficult is that you didn't study well enough (sorry to be so blunt). As demonstrated by Hermann Ebbinghaus long ago, there is no replacement for time spent learning. You must put in the time. There's no magic – just time.

Another reason exam questions are hard is that the material is complicated. Many courses are tough. Some stuff is just hard. A third possible explanation for why exam questions are difficult, one I have encountered frequently in my teaching experience, is that you may lack the needed college-level language ability. Any question is difficult if you don't have strong English language skills. Many teachers don't like telling you things like this because they think it is "politically incorrect" and might offend you. Well, I have no problem telling you the truth. Language skills matter, period. You will do yourself a huge favor if you choose to improve your vocabulary and grammar.

Over the years, I have had many conversations with students who are eager to learn how to study better. You can study for weeks but if the strategies you use are weak, you will find most exam questions are hard. The problem isn't the questions; it is how you studied. Yes, once again, this relates to *how you think*.

When teachers create exam questions, they have different goals in mind. At the most basic level, teachers want to make sure you know the basic concepts and definitions. However, questions can also ask you to explain things, use the concepts in real life examples, compare ideas, evaluate concepts and theories, and even develop and justify your own ideas or theories. Obviously, a question that asks you to evaluate a theory is more complicated than one that simply asks what the theory is.

In 1956, Benjamin Bloom published a taxonomy (a way of classifying things) that explained different levels of reasoning and thinking.[26] It can be considered "intellectual building blocks," ranging from simple to abstract.[27] Basically, Bloom realized that students have different levels of understanding when they learn something. For example, to understand a concept, you must first learn what the concept is. If an exam question asked you to understand a concept you had never heard of, you would likely get the question wrong.

Forty-five years later in 2001, Lorin Anderson and David Krathwohl updated Bloom's original taxonomy.[28]

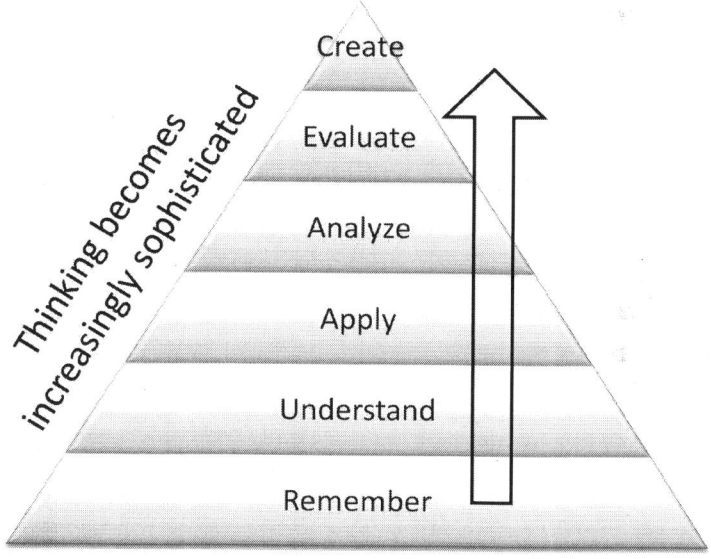

To appreciate your understanding of the material you study and the types of questions on an exam, let's look at the bottom three levels. The most basic level of thinking about the material you are learning is to simply remember it. Next, you try to understand it.

Once you understand it, you can apply it (use it) in new situations and examples.

Before we consider the top three levels of Bloom's taxonomy, let me share an important detail about applying your knowledge. Being able to apply what you're learning to real-life situations will increase your motivation to learn; an inability to apply the information to real life will decrease your motivation to learn the material.[29] That is why you should always write down examples given by the teacher. If none are given, ask.

The top three levels of the taxonomy represent higher levels of thinking about the material you are learning. The ability to analyze material requires you to organize, compare, and recognize relationships. To evaluate information, you must clearly explain and justify why you think it is good or bad, right or wrong. Finally, you should be able to use your new knowledge to create something original (or improve an existing idea).

I am sharing this so that you start to identify the difficulty level of exam questions and, therefore, prepare more effectively. If you only memorize your notes, you will only do well on exam questions that ask you to remember (the lowest level). If the exam has questions that require understanding, application, or more, you will do poorly with only the basics memorized. Therefore, it is important for you to adjust your studying to prepare yourself for questions at different levels of Bloom.

Professors in the biology department at the University of Washington developed something called BLASt (Bloom-based Learning Activities for Students).[30] They suggest different learning activities that can prepare you for questions at different levels of Bloom's taxonomy. For example, if you want to remember a concept, you can test yourself with flashcards. If you want to understand a concept, you should try summarizing it in your own words or try to explain it to others. To apply your knowledge, you should be able to come up with examples of a concept (or explain examples given to you). At the analysis level, you can compare and contrast ideas. To evaluate, you can identify the strengths and weaknesses of a theory. Finally, at the creating level you might try to design an experiment or develop a program.

Here is an awesome learning strategy suggestion: When you study, combine the use of Bloom's taxonomy with self-testing. Try to make up exam questions for the material you are studying, but make questions for each level of the taxonomy. I have given you an example of this in the chart below. It shows exam questions about the psychological concept of "negative reinforcement" for each level of the taxonomy. Start at the bottom and work your way up. You can see that the questions become more and more challenging the higher up you go. *Please read the chart. Do not skip it.*

Research has shown that making your own questions can help you understand the material better and do better on exams, especially if you are struggling with the material.[31] Creating (and then answering) questions about what you are studying makes you think more deeply about the material.[32]

Level of Bloom's Taxonomy	Example of an exam question for the level on the taxonomy
Create	Make up a lesson plan to teach a class of sixth graders about negative reinforcement.
Evaluate	In what situations might negative reinforcement be ineffective? Why?
Analyze	How is negative reinforcement different from negative punishment?
Apply	Give an example of how negative reinforcement can be used to encourage a child to eat broccoli.
Understand	Use your own words to describe the purpose of negative reinforcement.
Remember	Define negative reinforcement.

I understand that you might not have time to use the taxonomy for every single concept you are trying to learn in all your classes. As you read and study, however, please keep the taxonomy in mind. Remember metacognition? As you are studying and have the feeling of difficulty, you can now use Bloom's taxonomy to identify what the difficulty is. Are you having trouble understanding? Perhaps you understand the material but are having trouble applying it to different situations.

Here is an example (many students get stressed out by math questions like this): "Molly drives 60 mph for 4 hours, 70 mph for 2 hours, and 40 mph for 1 hour. What is Molly's average speed for her trip?"

Do you know the answer? In order to get the answer, you must first remember and understand that average speed is determined by dividing the total distance traveled by the total time for the trip. If you don't remember and understand that, you cannot apply it. You must also remember and understand basic addition, multiplication, and division. Then you must apply your knowledge to the question.

You can use Bloom's taxonomy to identify the thinking skills required for the type of question you're working on. That will allow you to modify your studying. This will go a long way when you need to overcome the metacognitive feeling of difficulty.

You can also use Bloom's taxonomy in class. For example, now that you know about it, you can see the importance of examples given during a lesson. They reflect the third level of the taxonomy and prepare you for application questions on exams (like the question about Molly's average speed). Students sometimes "tune out" when the teacher or professor gives examples. That is a *big* mistake. Always pay attention to and write down the examples. Depending on the type of class, you might discuss concepts in a group. That activity is designed to help you with the applying, analyzing, and evaluating levels of the taxonomy.

If you haven't noticed, here is the parallel between Bloom's taxonomy and college classes. Introductory, freshman classes are usually designed to help students with the first two or three levels of the taxonomy. For example, an Introductory Psychology course generally focuses on helping students remember and understand basic concepts. If it is a good course, like mine, it will also help students apply and analyze (levels 3 and 4) that information as well.

Any psychology classes you take after that should build on your existing knowledge and require you to think in more sophisticated ways about what you already learned. By the time you are finishing your bachelor's degree, and certainly if you are in graduate school, classes will require you to analyze, evaluate, and create more frequently than just remember and understand. The more advanced the classes are, the higher up the taxonomy your thinking should be.

A developmental psychologist named Lev Vygotsky talked about a concept known as scaffolding. Basically, he suggested that when students are first learning about something, they need a lot of help to remember and understand it. As students get more practice and become more knowledgeable, they need less help. The job of the teacher is to provide more support when students are new at something, and reduce the amount of support as students gain skill. That is scaffolding.

Now consider how this relates to Bloom's taxonomy. When you are first learning something, you might need a lot of help to understand it. The teacher's job is to provide you with the information and support you as you develop understanding. As you gain a stronger understanding, the teacher won't need to help you as much. The teacher can then push you to use the information and support you as you work through examples. Once you master application, the teacher can challenge you to develop the ability to analyze information. Are you seeing the relationship between teaching, learning, scaffolding, and Bloom's taxonomy?

Oh, by the way, did you figure out the answer to the question about Molly's average speed?

60mph x 4 hours	=	240 miles
70mph x 2 hours	=	140 miles
40mph x 1 hour	=	40 miles
———		———
7 hours		420 miles

Molly's average speed
*420 miles ÷ 7 hours = **60mph***

Advance Organizers

In Educational Psychology, advance organizers include any introductory material provided to students prior to a lesson that will help them connect what they already know to what is going to be taught. It has been suggested that the most important and meaningful aspect of learning is "consciously and explicitly relating new knowledge" to what you already know.[33] Advance organizers offer you a way to organize your thoughts and learning.[34,35,36] This can be something as simple as a teacher's outline of learning objectives before a lesson begins. However, this may not be the best kind of advance organizer because it makes you passive. That is, you just sit there and listen. A type of advance organizer that you can actively use without a teacher's help is called a KWL chart.

KWL Chart

Believe it or not, studying begins before you open a book or go to a class. The moment you think about a subject, the studying process starts. I know that sounds strange but bear with me. I'll do my best to explain.

Have you ever heard the saying, "prime the pump?" If not, this old saying basically means "getting something started." I am happy to tell you that there is an easy way to prime your studying and learning pump. All you have to do is ask yourself some basic questions before you study or go to class.

As you know, I teach psychology. What is psychology? What does a psychologist do? Why are some people mean? Why are some people nice? If you have questions like these in your mind before psychology class, you are already trying to learn psychology!

All your questions, curiosities, preconceived notions, and personal experiences are a great place to begin studying and learning.

These get you thinking about a topic before you ever try to learn about it. Just by asking, "What is psychology," you have directed your brain to think about psychology. As soon as you hear the definition in a lecture or read it in a textbook, your brain has an answer to something it was looking for. This immediately makes the information more meaningful. By asking the question, your brain is primed to find the answer. This is why textbooks and teachers state learning objectives. They are trying to make you curious. They are priming your brain for learning.

You can do this for yourself by using a KWL chart. KWL stands for "what do I **K**now, what do I **W**ant to know, and what did I **L**earn." It is a simple and brief exercise you can do before you read a chapter or listen to a lecture. You can fill out the first two columns of the chart before you read or attend class and then fill out the last column when you complete the reading or after class. Wow. There's another benefit of the KWL chart – you get to review and self-test at the end!

You just read about Bloom's Taxonomy. Do you remember how creating your own questions makes you think more deeply about the material? Do you remember the section on self-testing? I hope you see how all these strategies complement one another and help you achieve a much deeper level of learning.

Graphic Organizers/Concept Maps

Another form of advance organizer is something you have seen in textbooks and school before. Of course, you probably haven't been told for a long time about why they are important and many students fail to recognize them as a useful learning strategy.

Graphic organizers are a visual representation of related concepts. This is a great way to help make new and abstract ideas more concrete and, therefore, easier to remember and understand (the first two levels of Bloom).

Are you ready to be surprised? One of the most common forms of a graphic organizer is a simple flow chart (you know, concepts connected by arrows) that shows the relationships between and organization among concepts. Let me show you an example I just made up for demonstration. Please forgive the lack of scientific research in this case. See what you can learn just by looking at it. Yes, I want you to really look at it. *Please do not skip it.*

As you can see from the diagram, many things are related to academic success, including goals, motivation, interest, studying, and intelligence. Some are directly connected to success, such as studying. Other concepts are indirectly linked to success, such as how our goals influence motivation, which, in turn, leads to success. You can also see that some concepts are connected to each other in both directions. For example, motivation can lead to academic success but academic success also increases motivation.

By simply examining the concept map, you can learn a lot. Imagine if an instructor showed you this and the class discussed it *before* a lesson on academic success. It might help you organize your learning and develop a better, deeper understanding of the relationships between the concepts, not just learn the definitions of the concepts. Oh, and by the way, when you learn the relationships that exist between concepts, you are working at the fourth level of Bloom's taxonomy – analyze.

To Test or To Teach

In Key #1, I suggested that if you thought an exam was going to be oral, you'd probably study differently than if you were preparing for the usual written exam. Well, it should not surprise you that I have research to back me up!

In 2014, researchers did experiments where they had students study a passage for ten minutes and then take a test. All the students studied the same material, but some were told they would be taking a test about what they read, and others were told they would have to teach the material to someone else. Later, all the students were simply given the test (none actually had to teach). Can you guess what the researchers found? Students who thought they were going to teach the material to others did better on the test than students who simply prepared for the test. They showed better organization of ideas and remembered more of the main points.[37]

See, I am not making stuff up. When you are studying, it really is a good idea to prepare as if you will have to teach what you are learning to someone else. That strategy is more effective than just reading stuff over and over.

This shouldn't be surprising. Think for a second about your teachers and professors. Do you have any idea how much time it takes to prepare a lesson and know the material so well that we can answer all sorts of questions from students? Try doing what I do all the time when I prepare for classes with you – study like you are going to have to stand up in front of a bunch of people and teach. It is harder and takes more time, but you will really know your stuff!

Time Management

One of the most common concerns facing students these days is finding enough time to devote to school. There are so many competing demands, like family, friends, kids, and work, not to mention basics like self-care and time to have a little fun. With so much to do, it can be tough finding time to do homework and study.

College students today are different from the "traditional" students of previous generations. Now more than ever, students have many obligations outside of school. This is particularly true of first-generation students, those who are the first in their families to go to college. They work more hours and are often married and have children. This means they have to balance two conflicting worlds – traditional family roles and academic requirements. Unfortunately, there can be a lack of support for the latter leaving these students at higher risk for low achievement and even dropout.[38] As such, please know that I recognize the very real struggles of managing time when there are so many other things going on. Yet, if you are dealing with these challenges, time management is even more important. The benefits of good time management include better performance, less stress, and higher life satisfaction.[39]

The good news is that time management is a skill and is, therefore, something you can learn. Yet some of the skills that underlie time management are things most people don't talk about. Fortunately for you, some of what you've learned in the Psychological Keys to Student Success can be applied to time management.

Let's examine your beliefs (Key #1). If you believe there aren't enough hours in the day, you are basically confessing that you believe that time is the problem. You need to stop right there and change what you're telling yourself. Time is fine. This is all about *how you spend* your time. Here's another good metaphor: time and money are similar. The more you have, the more you spend. So, if we gave you more time, you would think there's plenty of it and would just waste more!

Another set of beliefs related to time has to do with priorities. Personally, I really don't like hearing people talk about "competing priorities." Look up the word priority and you'll see it means that one thing is regarded as more important than others. That means there is a hierarchy. If something is a priority, that means everything else must be second or third or tenth on the list. That means you have decisions to make. What is most important to you and, therefore, gets the most time? What is second? Third? Author Steven Covey once suggested that we should schedule our priorities instead of prioritizing all the stuff we write on our schedules.[40] Make sure your highest priorities are on your schedule every day.

Where does school fall in your priority hierarchy? If it is third or fourth or fifth on the list, you have your answer. If school isn't a top priority, it won't receive the time. And remember Hermann Ebbinghaus: *There is no replacement for time spent learning.* If you don't have the time to give, you won't do as well in school. That's it. Deal with the reality instead of saying you need more time. School is time-consuming and challenging. It is what it is.

Please understand that I am not judging you. I totally respect you for putting things like kids, family, and work at the top of the priority hierarchy. I'm simply asking you to be honest about the situation. I have a related piece of advice for you. You cannot be everything to everyone. If you try, you will burn out and be useless to your family, kids, and employer. Trying to do too much is, well, too much! If you feel like you just need a little more time, what you actually need is less stuff on your schedule. That might mean taking fewer classes, or cutting back on hours at work.

In Key #7, I told you about planning fallacy. That is the tendency to underestimate how much time you need to accomplish something. In order to overcome this problem, you need to be modest about your abilities and realistic about what has actually happened in the past. You know full well that the last paper took longer than you thought. *Learn from your experience!* You know that you should have dedicated more time to studying for that last exam. *Learn from your experience!* There is no magic needed here. You know what needs to happen. Either choose to do it or don't. But do not blame time.

Another common mistake related to time management is thinking you are a good multitasker. People's perception of their multitasking ability is very inflated.[41] The traditional view of multitasking is that it involves a person trying to do two independent activities that both require full awareness and attention. Clearly, in that situation, the tasks are actually competing for your attention. There is a long history of classic work on the limitations of our attention and the negative effect on our performance when we try to divide our attention.[42]

When it comes to doing two activities that require a lot of our attention, we are only ever doing one at a time. Did you "hear" that? We might flit quickly back and forth but, in any given second, we are only doing one task or the other. Interestingly, a trend in our society is heavy multimedia multitasking. Research has shown that people who frequently multitask using different sources of media are more distracted by irrelevant information and, hence, are actually worse at multitasking![43]

Research has also clearly demonstrated that we are "serial processors," meaning exactly what I just told you: We are only doing one thing at a time. Research by David Strayer has shown only a very small percentage of the population is able to do two cognitively demanding tasks at the same time and maintain accuracy in both.[44]

Without knowing it, you've learned a ton about time management already throughout this book:

- Develop a growth mindset and treat everything like it is a skill

- Be proactive and get ahead instead of falling behind and trying to catch up

- Break large assignments or studying for tests into small chunks.

- Review your progress

- Take breaks

- Ask for help

- Understand that failure is a learning experience, not a reason to put things off

- Use the incredibly awesome learning strategies - don't waste time reading and rereading

- Manage your learning environment (part of self-regulated learning) to eliminate distractions

- Don't fool yourself (planning fallacy)

Here are more reasons to develop and practice your time management skills. Research has shown that time management can actually protect you from the effects of stress and is a more effective stress-reducer than using time for leisure activities![45] Dealing effectively with stress, in part by managing time well, can reduce the tendency to procrastinate.[46]

FINAL THOUGHTS

There you have it – a handful of powerful learning strategies you can use to vastly improve your learning and success in college. The studying strategies used by most students are easier to use but they are less effective. With the commitment you've shown reading this book, I am confident that you are the student who wants to learn, not just study.

SECTION 4:
PSYCHOLOGICAL SKILLS

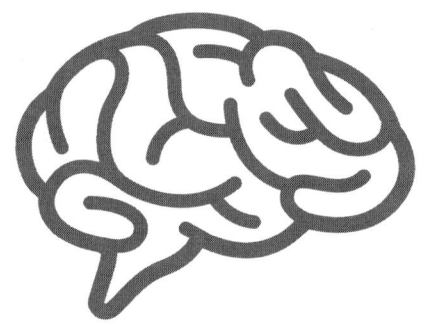

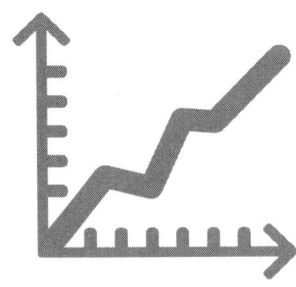

PERSONAL GROWTH AND SUCCESS

Psychological skills are essential to your education, academic success, and future well-being.

Thus far you have learned there are seven thinking skills (Keys) for student success, and that those keys are on a keychain called culture. You also have a newly developed portfolio of powerful learning strategies. Now I am going to add a notebook of five psychological skills to your educational backpack.

There is a song by Matchbox 20 called Long Day. I quote three lines of it for my classes each semester: "I'm so terrified of no one else but me. I'm here all the time. I won't go away."[1] Don't get hung up on the word "terrified." I use these lyrics to emphasize the fact that your thinking and your mental health both go with you everywhere, and they affect absolutely everything you do. It would be hard to walk around if you had an injured knee. Likewise, it is more difficult to be a successful student without certain psychological skills.

Based on over 20 years' experience in psychology, I believe there are core ideas from psychology that will help you not only be a better student, but become a happier, more fulfilled person. I am calling these ideas Psychological Skills. Remember, *you can learn* skills.

Emotional Intelligence

Emotional intelligence is something I call a "soft skill." It is hard to teach. Peter Salovey and John Mayer described it as "the ability to monitor one's own and others' feelings and emotions, to discriminate among them and to use this information to guide one's thinking and actions."[2] Psychologist Daniel Goleman wrote a book called *Emotional Intelligence* in 1995.[3] Helping students learn emotional (and social) skills has become a focus for schools since Goleman's book was published.

Emotional intelligence is made up of five main parts:

- Understanding your own emotions
- Managing your own emotions
- Recognizing and understanding the emotions of others
- Motivating yourself
- Handling relationships effectively

Research has demonstrated that higher emotional intelligence has many benefits. For example, one research study showed that college students in India with higher emotional intelligence experienced less stress.[4] In a study of Canadian college students, researchers discovered that emotional intelligence is associated with better adjustment to college which, in turn, helped students achieve higher first-year GPAs.[5] The benefits of developing social and emotional skills has also helped grade school students increase their academic achievement.[6]

Developing the personal and social skills associated with emotional intelligence is a clear benefit to you. One small tip I can give you is to practice listening for understanding. When someone finishes speaking, you should be able to accurately summarize both the content of what she said and the feelings associated with what she said. I always tell my students that you should listen for understanding, not just your chance to respond. Investing in others by truly listening is an emotional intelligence skill.

Because there is so much already written about emotional intelligence, I am not going to go into any further detail here. I am hoping that you will look into this more on your own and start developing the skills. It will help you in school, at work, and in your relationships.

Howard Gardner's Theory of Multiple Intelligences

In his book *Frames of Mind*, Howard Gardner suggested that there are seven different types of intelligence – linguistic, visual-spatial, logical-mathematical, bodily-kinesthetic, musical-rhythmic, interpersonal, and intrapersonal.[7] He later added naturalist intelligence for a total of eight intelligences.[8] Linguistic, visual-spatial, and logical-mathematical are the intelligences measured on conventional IQ tests. But we know there is more to intelligence than just IQ scores.

Here is a brief description of Gardner's eight intelligences *in terms of skills*:

- Linguistic – good with language, reading, writing, memorizing, and story-telling

- Visual-spatial – imagining objects in mind; mental rotation tasks; understanding direction

- Logical-mathematical – reasoning, logic, and critical thinking; math and computational skills

- Bodily-kinesthetic – balance, coordination, timing of movements; building things; skillful use of tools

- Musical-rhythmic – playing musical instruments; understanding and writing music; sense of pitch, melody, and rhythm

- Interpersonal – effective communication; empathy; working in groups; motivation

- Intrapersonal – self-awareness; self-motivation; evaluation of personal strengths and weaknesses

- Naturalist – understanding the natural environment and our impact on it; hunting/gathering/farming; classifying animals and plants

The important idea behind the theory of multiple intelligences is that most everything can be taught and learned in multiple ways. Gardner suggested that teachers should consider how their students process and learn information best. Just in case your instructors don't do that, I think you should do this for yourself. Consider the descriptions above, identify your skills, and think about how you can study and learn material using those skills.

A research study of first-year medical students found that two-thirds of the students preferred using multiple modes of learning.[9] For example, you could learn about fixing cars by reading manuals, watching videos, and through hands-on experience. Or, you could learn political theories by reading, making charts comparing party policies, debating, watching documentaries, or volunteering to support a local mayoral campaign. As you can see, there are multiple intelligences and learning styles at play, not just one.

Now think of Gardner's multiple intelligences in terms of learning skills and preferences. If you have higher bodily-kinesthetic intelligence, you might be a hands-on learner who wants to do practice problems or build/create something when you study. Or, if you learn best by interacting with others, you might be higher in interpersonal intelligence. Perhaps that means you should ask questions in class, participate in study groups, and practice explaining what you're learning to others.

Use Gardner's theory to explore your learning skills and preferred styles of learning. You don't want to waste time on studying strategies that don't fit your learning style.

The Stages of Change Model

The stages of change model[10] can help you understand how, when, and why people make changes (or don't) in their lives.[11] This is a great thing to know in terms of how you approach school and studying.

Here is a brief description of five of the six stages:

- Precontemplation – You have no intention of changing the (problem) behavior; you probably defend your current behavior by rationalizing and making excuses.

- Contemplation – You think about making a change but don't have a plan to actually change the (problem) behavior; you have made small, inconsistent attempts to change the behavior; you are considering the positive and negatives aspects of your current behavior; you feel ambivalent (i.e., torn, uncertain, uncommitted).

- Preparation – You are developing a plan to change your behavior and might have tried, in some small ways, to start the change; you might be researching strategies and ideas to help yourself.

- Action – You are actively changing your behavior and see the benefit of making the change.

- Maintenance – You have been able to keep the change you have made for a period of months and intend to continue with the new behavior; you make a plan for how to deal with setbacks and challenges to the new, healthier behavior

Now imagine for a moment why you bought my book. Did it look interesting? Did you have a bunch of spare change in your pocket? Or, was there a deeper reason? Maybe you recognized that something is missing in your approach to learning. Maybe you are motivated to develop better learning habits. Perhaps you are in the contemplation, preparation, or action stage of change. Now that you have read the descriptions of the stages and have considered your motivation for reading this book, what is your answer?

Using the stages of change model to assess your readiness for personal change is a fantastic psychological skill that promotes self-awareness and personal growth. If you would like a practical guide to making changes in your life, whether they are about school or other issues, I recommend *Changing For Good* by James Prochaska, John Norcross, and Carlo DiClemente.[12]

Effective Stress Management

Here is a wonderful metaphor about stress and how you deal with it: How can you tell what is inside an orange?

Squeeze it!

When you are "squeezed" (i.e., stressed), what comes out of you? Do you yell and scream? Cry? Withdraw? Reach out for help? Connect with others?

People have consistent ways of dealing with stress. Of course, there are situational differences, but personality psychology says we are predictable because we have behavioral tendencies. Personally, when I feel stressed, I tend to withdraw. I need time alone to consider possibilities and sort out my own thoughts. What about you? One of the stress management strategies I taught my clients, and one I tell students about, has to do with having good personal boundaries.

As a clinician, I worked with many single moms. I learned from them that they always put the needs of others first, and theirs last. They were most concerned with their kids – school, activities, homework, behavior, illnesses, special needs, having fun, etc. Otherwise, they were working, cooking, cleaning, shopping, doing laundry, mowing the lawn, shoveling snow, and paying bills. Many had no help from family. Some were new to the community and had not had time to make friends or connect with church or social services. Most described feeling stressed, overwhelmed, tired, and "at their wits' end."

The conversation I had with those dedicated, hard-working moms was, "If you 'break,' what will happen to your kids? If you fall apart because of stress, you won't be any good to anyone. Then what?" Those simple questions helped the moms understand a simple truth: You cannot be everything to everyone. Stress, in moderation, can improve your performance on some tasks. However, when stress is high and/or chronic, it can significantly limit your ability to do things well.

Why tell you that? One of the best stress management strategies I can offer you is to teach you an important word (one many people treat like it is a "bad" word). Ready?

NO

That's it. Your ability to say "No" is a good place to start when dealing with stress. When your sister calls and invites you shopping, but you have a big exam tomorrow, say no. If your boss asks you to work an extra shift but you have an assignment due, say no. If your friend just broke up with his/her sweetheart – you want to be supportive – but you're doing an online quiz, say no (and that you will call back when you're done).

It is hard to say no to people you care about. But it is a great skill. If you prefer to think about 'no' meaning 'not yet' or 'yes, later,' that's fine. Just make sure you establish the boundary. If our studying needs and school obligations are priorities, you *must* say no to others.

Another great stress management skill is to avoid known problem situations or people (sometimes called "source management").[13] Yes, avoidance. I am not telling you to pretend that stress doesn't exist. That would be called denial. I am telling you that, if you know the internet connection at home is unreliable, plan to use the computers at school or the library. If you know that traffic is bad in the morning, leave earlier. If you know a certain professor doesn't ever accept late work, do homework for that class first.

Here is a personal example: I live about 30 miles from school. When I teach a morning class that starts at 9 a.m, I leave my house at 6 a.m. Why? Traffic in the morning, between seven and eight, is horrible. If I left between those times, it would take me an hour or more to get to work. That could make me late, and would definitely make me cranky. Knowing the aggravation of morning traffic, I intentionally leave early and avoid traffic. This happens to come with two benefits – I get a lot of work done early in the day, and that means I often do not have to take work home in the evening.

Improving your time management skills is another great way to reduce stress. Time management is actually an example of something that requires a combination of the thinking skills, learning skills, and psychological skills you are learning. Throughout the thinking and learning skills sections, you have already learned many tips and techniques you can start using.

If you would like to read an interesting book about stress management, I recommend *The Stress-Proof Brain* by Melanie Greenberg.[14]

Perspective-taking

Al Haynes was a pilot who managed to fly a severely damaged commercial jet with nearly 300 passengers on board to an emergency landing. The damage to the plane was so bad that the pilots could not use conventional controls to turn it, make it go up or down, or use things like flaps and spoilers to slow it down. They had to figure out a way, using only power to the engines, to control the plane.

Instead of crashing in the middle of nowhere, their dedication, training, will, and skill got the plane to an airport. Sadly, the plane crash landed. Amazingly, because they got the plane to an airport where there were many emergency services waiting, nearly two-thirds of the people onboard survived, including all four pilots in the cockpit. (If you want to know more about this amazing story, I recommend *Flight 232: A Story of Disaster and Survival* by Laurence Gonzales.[15])

Imagine that you are Al Haynes. How would you feel? Are you happy that your efforts saved the lives of people who would have died otherwise? Or, would you feel guilty because many of the people on your plane died despite your greatest efforts? Would you be traumatized by the experience or would it reaffirm your identity as a good pilot?

Would you be surprised to learn that Al Haynes suffered from posttraumatic stress disorder (PTSD) after the crash? It did not surprise me. Given the circumstances, crash, and loss of life, it seems like stress and trauma are normal reactions to an unlikely and terrifying situation. Well, guess what. PTSD is a diagnosable mental disorder. It represents "abnormal" behavior.

I offer that story to show you the importance of perspective. Compared to what Al Haynes experienced, his reaction seems very understandable to me. If he ended up with PTSD because he stubbed his toe, that would be abnormal. Understanding what is normal or abnormal requires us to consider the context – the situation. You already learned how important the context is when you learned how culture influences the seven Key thinking skills!

Here is another neat idea I share with my classes about perspective-taking. There is an Eastern philosophy called Taoism. One of the things it does is show how opposites are, as a matter of fact, often closely linked. Try this activity: Take a blank piece of paper and turn it sideways (i.e., landscape). Draw a straight line across the page with the words "good" and "bad" at opposite ends of the line. Actually, the line could be squiggly; as long as good and bad, which are opposites, are at opposite ends of the line, the shape of the line doesn't matter.

Given that the shape of the line doesn't matter, pick up the piece of paper and curve it into a cylinder. Now the line is curved but, not only are good and bad at opposite ends of the line, they are also sitting right next to each other! For example, have you ever told the truth but really hurt someone's feelings? On the other hand, have you ever broken the rules (e.g., come home late) and actually done the right thing in the process (e.g., helped an intoxicated friend get home safely)?

Sometimes two things that appear to be completely different are really very much alike. Another example of this involves love and hate. Some people consider those emotions to be opposites. However, both are intense, require great emotional energy, and focus you on a specific person. The opposite of both love and hate is actually indifference.

My point here is that there is always another way to understand something. The way you interpret things is your perspective. Your perspective is only one perspective in a world of over 7.5 billion perspectives! Remember that the next time you are convinced you are "right."

FINAL THOUGHTS

The psychological skills described influence how and what you learn, so schools, students, and families should help students and educators address such issues.[16] I feel very strongly that these psychological skills are essential to your success. Not all teachers or schools will emphasize them as part of your education, academic success, and future well-being. I want you to do well and be well. Please pursue the skills on your own now that you have learned of their importance.

THANK YOU

What I have shared with you in this book is my perspective. I have supported it with decades of research and over 20 years of clinical and teaching experience. What matters now is how you use the information to develop your own personal approach to learning.

Thank you for sharing your time with me. Thank you for the effort you made reading this book. Thank you for the opportunity to be a part of your educational journey. It is my sincere hope that the information and ideas will be a positive influence as you move forward in school, and life. To you and your family, present and future, I wish you the very best.

Troy Dvorak

RockinPsychProf (Facebook)
www.psychologyrocks.com

NOTES

Are You Learning, or Just Studying?

[1] Weinstein, C. E., and Meyer, D. K. (1994). Learning strategies, teaching and testing. *The International Encyclopedia of Education, 6,* 3335-40.

[2] Quotation from page 7 of Gall, M.D., Gall, J. P., Jacobsen, D. R., and Bullock, T. L. (1990). *Tools for learning: A guide to teaching study skills.* Alexandria, VA: Association for Supervision and Curriculum Development.

[3] Research by Chapel (1995) as cited on page 172 of Weissberg, N. C., Owen, D. R., Jenkins, A. H., and Harburg, E. (2003). The incremental variance problem: Enhancing the predictability of academic success in an urban, commuter institution. *Genetic, Social, and General Psychology Monographs, 129*(2), 153-180.

[4] Kena, G., Hussar, W., McFarland, J., de Brey, C., Musu-Gillette, L., Wang, X., and Ossolinski, M. (2016). *Conditions of education 2016: Racial/ethnic enrollment in public schools (NCES 2016144).* US Department of Education, National Center for Education Statistics. Washington, DC.

[5] Lotkowski, V. A., Robbins, S. B., and Noeth, R. J. (2004). The role of academic and non academic factors in improving college retention. ACT Policy Report. *American College Testing ACT Inc.*

[6] Brown, S. D., Tramayne, S., Hoxha, D., Telander, K., Fan, X., and Lent, R. W. (2008). Social cognitive predictors of college students' academic performance and persistence: A meta-analytic path analysis. *Journal of Vocational Behavior, 72*(3), 298-308.

[7] Pascarella, E. T., Wolniak, G. C., and Pierson, C. T. (2003). Influences on community college students' educational plans. *Research in Higher Education, 44*(3), 301-314.

[8] The predictors of academic success are many and are complex. General cognitive ability (intelligence) is, undeniably, one of those factors. There is a tome of research in that area and it was not my intention to review it in this book. However, for some interesting examples, one might consider Kuncel, N. R., Hezlett, S. A., and Ones, D. S. (2004). Academic performance, career potential, creativity, and job performance: Can one construct predict them all? *Journal of Personality and Social Psychology, 86*(1), 148. Another interesting study is Furnham, A. (2012). Learning styles, personality traits and intelligence as predictors of college academic performance. *Individual Differences Research, 10*(3), 117-128. See also Higgins, D. M., Peterson, J. B., Pihl, R. O., and Lee, A. G. (2007). Prefrontal cognitive ability, intelligence, Big Five personality, and the prediction of advanced academic and workplace performance. *Journal of Personality and Social Psychology, 93*(2), 298-319. For consideration of "academic ability" and its relationship to achievement, see Harackiewicz, J. M., Barron, K. E., Tauer, J. M., and Elliot, A. J. (2002). Predicting success in college: A longitudinal study of achievement goals and ability measures as predictors of interest and performance from freshman year through graduation. *Journal of Educational Psychology, 94*(3), 562-575.

[9] Thank you to Elaine Hauff, an extraordinary educator and person, for her commitment to students. It is my pleasure to know her and call her a friend.

[10] Duckworth, A. L., Quinn, P. D., and Tsukayama, E. (2012). What No Child Left Behind leaves behind: The roles of IQ and self-control in predicting standardized achievement test scores and report card grades. *Journal of Educational Psychology, 104*(2), 439-451.

[11] Quotation from page 359 of Cornford, I. R. (2002). Learning-to-learn strategies as a basis for effective lifelong learning. *International Journal of Lifelong Education, 21*(4), 357-368.

[12] For example, see Sparkman, L., Maulding, W., & Roberts, J. (2012). Non-cognitive predictors of student success in college. *College Student Journal, 46*(3), 642-652.

Your Learning Objectives

[1] Talmor, R., Kayam, O., Shoval, E., and Galily, Y. (2013). Success is a choice! Explaining success in academic preparation programs in Israel. *Journal of Comparative Research in Anthropology and Sociology, 4*(1), 141-150.

[2] Corno, L., and Mandinach, E. B. (2004). What we have learned about student engagement in the past twenty years. In Dennis M. McInerney and Shawn Van Etten (Eds.), *Big Theories Revisited* (Vol. 4; pp. 297-326). USA: Information Age Publishing.

[3] McKenzie, K., Gow, K., and Schweitzer, R. (2004). Exploring first-year academic achievement through structural equation modelling. *Higher Education Research & Development, 23*(1), 95-112.

[4] Stupnisky, R. H., Renaud, R. D., Daniels, L. M., Haynes, T. L., and Perry, R. P. (2008). The interrelation of first-year college students' critical thinking disposition, perceived academic control, and academic achievement. *Research in Higher Education, 49*(6), 513-530.

[5] You, S., Hong, S., and Ho, H. Z. (2011). Longitudinal effects of perceived control on academic achievement. *Journal of Educational Research, 104*(4), 253-266.

[6] Fishman, E. J. (2014). With great control comes great responsibility: The relationship between perceived academic control, student responsibility, and self-regulation. *British Journal of Educational Psychology, 84*(4), 685-702.

[7] Pekrun, R., Goetz, T., Perry, R. P., Kramer, K., Hochstadt, M., and Molfenter, S. (2004). Beyond test anxiety: Development and validation of the Test Emotions Questionnaire (TEQ). *Anxiety, Stress & Coping, 17*(3), 287-316.

[8] Perry, R. P., Hladkyj, S., Pekrun, R. H., and Pelletier, S. T. (2001). Academic control and action control in the achievement of college students: A longitudinal field study. *Journal of educational psychology, 93*(4), 776-789.

[9] Perry, R. P., Hladkyj, S., Pekrun, R. H., Clifton, R. A., and Chipperfield, J. G. (2005). Perceived academic control and failure in college students: A three-year study of scholastic attainment. *Research in Higher Education, 46*(5), 535-569.

[10] Ruthig, J. C., Haynes, T. L., Stupnisky, R. H., and Perry, R. P. (2009). Perceived academic control: Mediating the effects of optimism and social support on college students' psychological health. *Social Psychology of Education, 12*(2), 233-249.

[11] Haynes, T. L., Perry, R. P., Stupnisky, R. H., and Daniels, L. M. (2009). A review of attributional retraining treatments: Fostering engagement and persistence in vulnerable college students. In *Higher education: Handbook of theory and research* (pp. 227-272). Springer Netherlands.

[12] List of resiliency factors found in Kitano, M. K., and Lewis, R. B. (2005). Resilience and coping: Implications for gifted children and youth at risk. *Roeper Review, 27*(4), 200-205.

[13] Credé, M., and Kuncel, N. R. (2008). Study habits, skills, and attitudes: The third pillar supporting collegiate academic performance. *Perspectives on Psychological Science, 3*(6), 425-453.

[14] Kappe, R., and Van der Flier, H. (2012). Predicting academic success in higher education: what's more important than being smart?. *European Journal of Psychology of Education, 27*(4), 605-619.

[15] Duckworth, A. L., Peterson, C., Matthews, M. D., and Kelly, D. R. (2007). Grit: perseverance and passion for long-term goals. *Journal of Personality and Social Psychology, 92*(6), 1087-1101.

[16] Duckworth, A. (2016). Grit: The power of passion and perseverance. Simon and Schuster.

[17] Barbatis, P. (2010). Underprepared, ethnically diverse community college students: Factors contributing to persistence. *Journal of Developmental Education, 33*(3), 14-26.

[18] Lauermann, F., and Karabenick, S. A. (2011). Taking teacher responsibility into account (ability): Explicating its multiple components and theoretical status. *Educational Psychologist, 46*(2), 122-140.

[19] The Carnegie Foundation for the Advancement of Teaching. (2011). *Productive persistence: Overview of productive persistence starter package*. Version 1.5. Retrieved from http://www.tlok.org/statway/Productive%20Persistence%20Starter%20Package%20Overview.pdf

Motivation – The Beginning

[1] Quotation from pages 80-81 of Murray, H. A. (1938). *Explorations in Personality*. New York: Oxford University Press.

[2] For more explanation of these ideas, see McClelland, D. C., Atkinson, J. W., Clark, R. A., and Lowell, E. L. (1953). *The Achievement Motive.* New York: Appleton–Century–Crofts.

[3] For more explanation of these ideas, see Atkinson, J. W. (1957). Motivational determinants of risk-taking behavior. *Psychological Review, 64*, 359-372.

[4] Elliot, A. J., and Sheldon, K. M. (1997). Avoidance achievement motivation: A personal goals analysis. *Journal of Personality and Social Psychology, 73*(1), 171-185.

[5] For example, see Martin, A. J., Marsh, H. W., and Debus, R. L. (2001). Self-handicapping and defensive pessimism: Exploring a model of predictors and outcomes from a self-protection perspective. *Journal of Educational Psychology, 93*(1), 87-102.

[6] For example, see Thompson, T., Davidson, J. A., and Barber, J. G. (1995). Self-worth protection in achievement motivation: Performance effects and attributional behavior. *Journal of Educational Psychology, 87*(4), 598-610.

[7] Covington, M. V. (2000). Goal theory, motivation, and school achievement: An integrative review. *Annual Review of Psychology, 51*(1), 171-200.

[8] Ajzen, I. (1991). The theory of planned behavior. *Organizational Behavior and Human Decision Processes, 50*, 179-211.

[9] Deci, E. L., and Ryan, R. M. (1987). The support of autonomy and the control of behavior. *Journal of Personality and Social Psychology, 53*(6), 1024-1037.

[10] Deci, E. L., and Ryan, R. M. (1987).

[11] Deci, E. L., and Ryan, R. M. (1987).

[12] Deci, E. L, Koestner, R., and Ryan, R. M. (1999). A meta-analytic review of experiments examining the effects of extrinsic rewards on intrinsic motivation. *Psychological Bulletin, 125*(6), 627-668.

[13] Quotation from page 190 of Wolters, C. A. (2003). Regulation of motivation: Evaluating an underemphasized aspect of self-regulated learning. *Educational Psychologist, 38*(4), 189-205.

[14] Lazowski, R. A., and Hulleman, C. S. (2016). Motivation Interventions in Education: A Meta-Analytic Review. Review of Educational Research, 86(2), 602-640.

Key #1: Beliefs & Mindset

[1] Quotation from page 11 of Perna, L. W., and Thomas, S. L. (2006, July). A framework for reducing the college success gap and promoting success for all. In *National Symposium on Postsecondary Student Success: Spearheading a Dialog on Student Success (pp 1-42).*

[2] Parpala, A., Lindblom-Ylänne, S., Komulainen, E., Litmanen, T., and Hirsto, L. (2010). Students' approaches to learning and their experiences of the teaching–learning environment in different disciplines. *British Journal of Educational Psychology, 80*(2), 269-282.

[3] Cornford, I. R. (2002). Learning-to-learn strategies as a basis for effective lifelong learning. *International Journal of Lifelong Education, 21*(4), 357-368.

[4] Schommer, M. (1993). Comparisons of beliefs about the nature of knowledge and learning among postsecondary students. *Research in Higher Education, 34*(3), 355-370.

[5] Dahl, T. I., Bals, M., and Turi, A. L. (2005). Are students' beliefs about knowledge and learning associated with their reported use of learning strategies? *British Journal of Psychology, 75*(2), 257-273.

[6] Schommer, M. (1990). Effects of beliefs about the nature of knowledge on comprehension. *Journal of Educational Psychology, 82*(3), 498-504.

[7] Schommer, M. (1993).

[8] Schommer, M., and Walker, K. (1997). Epistemological beliefs and valuing school: Considerations for college admissions and retention. *Research in Higher Education, 38*(2), 173-186.

[9] Quotation from page 269 of Dahl, T. I., et al., (2005).

[10] Phan, H. P. (2009). Amalgamation of future time orientation, epistemological beliefs, achievement goals and study strategies: Empirical evidence established. *British Journal of Educational Psychology, 79*(1), 155-173.

[11] Wyre, S. H. (2012). Metacognitive Enrichment for Community College Students. *Community College Journal of Research and Practice, 36(12)*, 994-1003.

[12] Grimes, P. W. (2002). The overconfident principles of economics student: An examination of a metacognitive skill. *The Journal of Economic Education, 33*(1), 15-30.

[13] For example, see Pekrun, R., Goetz, T., Titz, W., and Perry, R. P. (2002). Academic emotions in students' self-regulated learning and achievement: A program of quantitative and qualitative research. *Educational Psychologist, 37*, 91–106.

[14] Ross, M. E., Green, S. B., Salisbury-Glennon, J. D., and Tollefson, N. (2006). College students' study strategies as a function of testing: An investigation into metacognitive self-regulation. *Innovative Higher Education, 30*(5), 361-375.

[15] Entwistle, N., and Entwistle, D. (2003). Preparing for examinations: The interplay of memorising and understanding, and the

development of knowledge objects. *Higher Education Research and Development, 22*(1), 19-41.

[16] Karpicke, J. D., Butler, A. C., and Roediger III, H. L. (2009). Metacognitive strategies in student learning: Do students practise retrieval when they study on their own? *Memory, 17*(4), 471-479.

[17] Quotation from page 432 of Collier, P. J., and Morgan, D. L. (2008). Is that paper really due today?: Differences in first-generation and traditional college students' understanding of faculty expectations. *Higher Education, 55*(4), 425-446.

[18] Valentine, J. C., DuBois, D. L., and Cooper, H. (2004). The relation between self-beliefs and academic achievement: A meta-analytic review. *Educational Psychologist, 39*(2), 111-133.

[19] Quotation from page 189 of Ajzen, I. (1991). The theory of planned behavior. *Organizational Behavior and Human Decision Processes, 50*(2), 179-211.

[20] Molden, D. C., and Dweck, C. S. (2006). Finding" meaning" in psychology: a lay theories approach to self-regulation, social perception, and social development. *American Psychologist, 61*(3), 192.

[21] Molden, D. C., and Dweck, C. S. (2006).

[22] Mindset Works Inc. (2016). You can grow your intelligence. http://www.mindsetworks.com/FileCenter/52G3LTP08OVNI3G9NMI8.pdf

[23] Moser, J. S., Schroder, H. S., Heeter, C., Moran, T. P., and Lee, Y. H. (2011). Mind your errors: Evidence for a neural mechanism linking growth mindset to adaptive posterror adjustments. *Psychological Science, 22*(12),1484-1489.

[24] Maguire, E., K. Woollett and H. Spiers. (2006). London taxi drivers and bus drivers: A structural MRI and neuropsychological analysis. *Hippocampus, 16*(12), 1091-1101.

[25] Blackwell, L. S., Trzesniewski, K. H., and Dweck, C. S. (2007). Implicit theories of intelligence predict achievement across an adolescent transition: A longitudinal study and an intervention. *Child Development, 78*(1), 246-263.

[26] Quotation from page 105 of Boekaerts, M. (1996). Self-regulated learning at the junction of cognition and motivation. *European Psychologist, 1*(2), 100-112.

[27] Conley (2007), as cited in Roderick, M., Coca, V., and Nagaoka, J. (2011). Potholes on the road to college. High school effects in shaping urban students' participation in college application, four-year college enrollment, and college match. Sociology of Education, 84(3), 178-211.

Key #2: Attributions

[1] Quotation from page 3 of Weiner, B. (1979). A theory of motivation for some classroom experiences. *Journal of Educational Psychology, 71*(1), 3-25.

[2] S33 page 4 of Weiner, B. (1979).

[3] Weiner, B. (1979).

[4] Shell, D. F., and Husman, J. (2008). Control, motivation, affect, and strategic self-regulation in the college classroom: A multidimensional phenomenon. *Journal of Educational Psychology, 100*(2), 443-459.

[5] Perry, R. P., Hladkyj, S., Pekrun, R. H., and Pelletier, S. T. (2001). Academic control and action control in the achievement of college

students: A longitudinal field study. *Journal of Educational Psychology, 93*(4), 776-789.

[6] Perry, R. P. (2003). Perceived (academic) control and causal thinking in achievement settings. *Canadian Psychology, 44*(4), 312-331.

[7] Linnenbrink, E. A., and Pintrich, P. R. (2002). Motivation as an enabler for academic success. *School Psychology Review, 31*(3), 313-327.

[8] Rotter, J. B. (1966). Generalized expectancies for internal versus external control of reinforcement. *Psychological Monographs: General and Applied, 80*(1), 1-28.

[9] According to Weiner, B. (1985). An attributional theory of achievement motivation and emotion. *Psychological Review, 92*(4), 548-573, this is common.

[10] Heider, F. (1958). *The psychology of interpersonal relations.* New York: Wiley.

[11] Rotter, J. B. (1966). Generalized expectancies for internal versus external control of reinforcement. *Psychological monographs: General and applied, 80*(1), 1-28.

[12] Atkinson, J. W. (1964). *An introduction to motivation.* Princeton, N.J.: Van Nostrand.

[13] Weiner (1985).

[14] Weiner (2010).

[15] Schunk, D. H., Meece, J. L., and Pintrich, P. R. (2014). *Motivation in education: Theory, research, and applications* (4th ed.). Upper Saddle River, NJ: Pearson.

[16] For a review, see Haynes, T. L. et. al. (2009).

[17] Boese, G. D., Stewart, T. L., Perry, R. P., and Hamm, J. M. (2013). Assisting failure-prone individuals to navigate achievement transitions using a cognitive motivation treatment (attributional retraining). *Journal of Applied Social Psychology, 43*(9), 1946-1955.

[18] Hamm, J. M., Perry, R. P., Clifton, R. A., Chipperfield, J. G., and Boese, G. D. (2014). Attributional retraining: A motivation treatment with differential psychosocial and performance benefits for failure prone individuals in competitive achievement settings. *Basic and Applied Social Psychology, 36*(3), 221-237.

[19] Haynes, T. L., Daniels, L. M., Stupnisky, R. H., Perry, R. P., and Hladkyj, S. (2008). The effect of attributional retraining on mastery and performance motivation among first-year college students. *Basic and Applied Social Psychology, 30*(3), 198-207.

[20] Perry, R. P., and Penner, K. S. (1990). Enhancing academic achievement in college students through attributional retraining and instruction. *Journal of Educational Psychology, 82*(2), 262-271.

[21] Perry, R. P., and Struthers, C. W. (1994, April). Attributional retraining in the college classroom: Some causes for optimism. In American Educational Research Association annual meeting, New Orleans, LA.

[22] For a review, see Haynes, T. L. et. al. (2009).

[23] Radcliffe, N. M., and Klein, W. M. (2002). Dispositional, unrealistic, and comparative optimism: Differential relations with the knowledge and processing of risk information and beliefs about personal risk. *Personality and Social Psychology Bulletin, 28*(6), 836-846.

[24] Overwalle, F., and de Metsenaere, M. (1990). The effects of attribution-based intervention and study strategy training on academic achievement in college freshmen. *British Journal of Educational Psychology, 60*(3), 299-311.

[25] Covington, M. V. (1984). The self-worth theory of achievement motivation: Findings and implications. *The Elementary School Journal, 85*(1), 5-20.

Key #3: Achievement Goals & Interest

[1] Quotation from page 215 of Urdan, T. C., and Maehr, M. L. (1995). Beyond a two-goal theory of motivation and achievement: A case for social goals. *Review of Educational Research, 65*(3), 213-243.

[2] Wentzel, K. R. (2000). What is it that I'm trying to achieve? Classroom goals from a content perspective. *Contemporary Educational Psychology, 25*, 105-115.

[3] Miller, R. B., and Brickman, S. J. (2004). A model of future-oriented motivation and self-regulation. *Educational Psychology Review, 16*(1), 9-33.

[4] Hulleman, C. S., Schrager, S. M., Bodmann, S. M., and Harackiewicz, J. M. (2010). A meta-analytic review of achievement goal measures: Different labels for the same constructs or different constructs with similar labels? *Psychological Bulletin, 136*(3), 422-449.

[5] Quotation from page 261 of Ames, C. (1992). Classrooms: Goals, structures, and student motivation. *Journal of Educational Psychology, 84*(3), 261-271.

[6] Quotation from page 423 of Hulleman, et. al. (2010).

[7] Pintrich, P. (2000). An achievement goal theory perspective on issues in motivation terminology, theory, and research. *Contemporary Educational Psychology, 25*(1), 92–104.

[8] Ideas in this paragraph are based on Dweck, C. S., and Leggett, E. L. (1988). A social-cognitive approach to motivation and personality. *Psychological Review, 95*, 256–273.

[9] Senko, C., Hulleman, C. S., and Harackiewicz, J. M. (2011). Achievement goal theory at the crossroads: Old controversies, current challenges, and new directions. *Educational Psychologist, 46*(1), 26-47.

[10] Covington, M. V. (2000). Goal theory, motivation, and school achievement: An integrative review. *Annual Review of Psychology, 51*(1), 171-200.

[11] Quotation from page 194 of Schunk, D. H., Meece, J. L., and Pintrich, P. R. (2014). *Motivation in Education* (4th ed.). Upper Saddle River, NJ: Pearson.

[12] Grant, H. and Dweck, C. S. (2003). Clarifying achievement goals and their impact. *Journal of Personality and Social Psychology, 85,* 541-553.

[13] Weiner, B. (1979). A theory of motivation for some classroom experiences. *Journal of Educational Psychology, 71*(1), 3-25.

[14] Ames, C. (1992).

[15] Hulleman, et. al. (2010).

[16] Senko, C., et. al. (2011).

[17] Pekrun R., Elliot, A. J., and Maier, M. A. (2009). Achievement goals and achievement emotions: Testing a model of their joint relations with academic performance. *Journal of Educational Psychology, 101*(1), 115-135.

[18] Hulleman, et. al. (2010).

[19] Baumeister, R. F., Bratslavsky, E., Finkenauer, C., and Vohs, K. D. (2001). Bad is stronger than good. *Review of General Psychology, 5*(4), 323-370.

[20] Elliot, A. J., and Harackiewicz, J. M. (1996). Approach and avoidance achievement goals and intrinsic motivation: A mediational analysis. *Journal of Personality and Social Psychology, 70*, 461-475.

[21] Quotation from page 186 of Covington, M. V. (2000).

[22] Research conducted by Senko and Harackiewicz as cited in Brophy, J. (2005). Goal theorists should move on from performance goals. *Educational Psychologist, 40*(3), 167-176.

[23] Elliot, A. J., and Church, M. A. (1997). A hierarchical model of approach and avoidance achievement motivation. *Journal of Personality and Social Psychology,72*(1), 218-232.

[24] Covington, M. V. (2000).

[25] Pekrun R., et. al. (2009).

[26] Harackiewicz, J. M., Barron, K. E., Tauer, J. M., and Elliot, A. J. (2002). Predicting success in college: A longitudinal study of achievement goals and ability measures as predictors of interest and performance from freshman year through graduation. *Journal of Educational Psychology, 94*(3), 562-575.

[27] Jennings, N., Lovett, S., Cuba, L., Swingle, J., and Lindkvist, H. (2013). "What would make this a successful year for you?" How students define success in college. *Liberal Education, Spring 2013*, 40-47.

[28] Pintrich, P. R. (2003). A motivational science perspective on the role of student motivation in learning and teaching contexts. *Journal of Educational Psychology, 95*(4), 667-686.

[29] Research by Rathunde as cited in Hidi, S., and Harackiewicz, J. M. (2000). Motivating the academically unmotivated: A critical issue for the 21st century. *Review of Educational Research, 70*(2), 151-179.

[30] For a review, see Hidi, S., and Harackiewicz, J. M. (2000).

[31] For a review, see Renninger, K. A., and Hidi, S. (2011). Revisiting the conceptualization, measurement, and generation of interest. *Educational Psychologist, 46*(3), 168-184.

[32] Mitchell, M. (1993). Situational interest: Its multifaceted structure in the secondary school mathematics classroom. *Journal of Educational Psychology, 85*(3), 424-436.

[33] For example, see Hulleman, C. S., Godes, O., Hendricks, B. L., and Harackiewicz, J. M. (2010). Enhancing interest and performance with a utility value intervention. *Journal of Educational Psychology, 102*(4), 880-895.

[34] Mitchell, M. (1993).

[35] Azevedo, R. (2005). Using hypermedia as a metacognitive tool for enhancing student learning? The role of self-regulated learning. *Educational Psychologist, 40*(4), 199-209.

[36] Son, L. K., and Metcalfe, J. (2000). Metacognitive and control strategies in study-time allocation. *Journal of Experimental Psychology: Learning, Memory, and Cognition, 26*(1), 204-221.

[37] Boekaerts, M., and Corno, L. (2005). Self-regulation in the classroom: A perspective on assessment and intervention. *Applied Psychology: An International Review, 54*(2), 199-231.

Key #4: Self-efficacy

[1] Eccles, J. S., and Wigfield, A. (2002). Motivational beliefs, values, and goals. *Annual Review of Psychology, 53*, 109-132.

[2] Dennison, J. J. A., Zarrett, N. R., and Eccles, J. S. (2007). I like to do it, I'm able, and I know I am: Longitudinal couplings between domain-specific achievement, self-concept, and interest. *Child Development, 78*(2), 430-447.

[3] Zimmerman, B. J. (1995). Self-regulation involves more than metacognition: A social cognitive perspective. *Educational Psychologist, 30*(4), 217-221.

[4] Pintrich, P. R. (2003). A motivational science perspective on the role of student motivation in learning and teaching contexts. *Journal of Educational Psychology, 95*(4), 667-686.

[5] Pajares, F. (2002). Gender and perceived self-efficacy in self-regulated learning. *Theory Into Practice, 41*(2), 116-125.

[6] Pintrich, P.R. (2003).

[7] Zimmerman, B. J. and Cleary, T. J. (2006). Adolescents' development of personal agency: The role of self-efficacy beliefs and self-regulatory skill. In F. Pajares and T. Urdan (Eds.), *Self-efficacy beliefs of adolescents* (pp. 45-70). Greenwich, CT: Information Age Publishing.

[8] "Selection processes," paragraph 1 of Bandura, A. (1994). Self-efficacy. In V. S. Ramachaudran (Ed.). *Encyclopedia of human behavior* (Vol. 4, pp. 71-81). New York: Academic Press. Retrieved from http://www.uky.edu/~eushe2/Bandura/BanEncy.html

[9] Quotation from page 542 of Cleary, T. J., and Zimmerman, B. J. (2004). Self-regulation empowerment program: A school-based program to enhance self-regulated and self-motivated cycles of student learning. *Psychology in the Schools, 41*(5), 537-550.

[10] Multon, K. D., Brown, S. D., & Lent, R. W. (1991). Relation of self-efficacy beliefs to academic outcomes: A meta-analytic investigation. Journal of counseling psychology, 38(1), 30.

[11] Robbins, S. B., Lauver, K., Le, H., Davis, D., Langley, R., and Carlstrom, A. (2004). Do psychosocial and study skill factors predict college outcomes? A meta-analysis. *Psychological Bulletin, 130*(2), 261.

[12] Bandura, A. (1977). Self-efficacy: Toward a unifying theory of behavioral change. *Psychological Review, 84*(2), 191-215.

[13] Quotation on page 195 of Bandura, A. (1977).

[14] Quotation on page 27 of Miller, R. B., and Brickman, S. J. (2004). A model of future-oriented motivation and self-regulation. *Educational Psychology Review, 16*(1), 9-33.

[15] Weiner, B. (1979). A theory of motivation for some classroom experiences. *Journal of Educational Psychology, 71*(1), 3-25.

[16] Bandura, A. (1977).

[17] For an example of an empirical study demonstrating the effect of watching non-experts perform a behavior on another's self-efficacy, see Schunk, D. H., and Hanson, A. R. (1985). Peer models: Influence on children's self-efficacy and achievement. *Journal of Educational Psychology, 77*, 313-322.

[18] Bandura, A. (1994). Self-efficacy. In V. S. Ramachaudran (Ed.). *Encyclopedia of human behavior* (Vol. 4, pp. 71-81). New York: Academic Press. Retrieved from http://www.uky.edu/~eushe2/Bandura/BanEncy.html

[19] Senko, C., Hulleman, C. S., and Harackiewicz, J. M. (2011). Achievement goal theory at the crossroads: Old controversies, current challenges, and new directions. *Educational Psychologist, 46*(1), 26-47.

[20] Quotation on page 315 of Linnenbrink, E. A., and Pintrich, P. R. (2002). Motivation as an enabler for academic success. *School Psychology Review, 31*(3), 313-327.

[21] Schunk, D. H. (1991). Self-efficacy and academic motivation. *Educational Psychologist, 26*(3&4), 207-231.

[22] Zimmerman, B. J. and Cleary, T. J. (2006).

[23] Zimmerman, B. J. and Cleary, T. J. (2006).

[24] Schraw, G., Crippen, K. J., and Hartley, K. (2006). Promoting self-regulation in science education: Metacognition as part of a broader perspective on learning. *Research in Science Education, 36,* 111-139.

[25] Pintrich, P.R. (2003).

[26] Corno, L., and Mandinach, E. B. (2004). What we have learned about student engagement in the past twenty years. In Dennis M. McInerney and Shawn Van Etten (Eds.), *Big Theories Revisited* (Vol. 4; pp. 297-326). USA: Information Age Publishing.

[27] Brophy, J. (2005). Goal theorists should move on from performance goals. *Educational Psychologist, 40*(3), 167-176.

[28] Locke, E. A., and Latham, G. P. (2002). Building a practically useful theory of goal setting and task motivation: A 35-year odyssey. *American Psychologist, 57*(9), 705–717.

[29] Some of the suggestions are based on Siegle, D., and McCoach, D. B. (2007). Increasing student mathematics self-efficacy through teacher training. *Journal of Advanced Academics, 18*(2), 278-312.

Key #5: Metacognition

[1] Quotation from page 136 of Lew, M. D. N., Alwis, W. A. M., and Schmidt, H. G. (2010). Accuracy of students' self-assessment and their beliefs about its utility. *Assessment & Evaluation in Higher Education, 35*(2), 135-156.

[2] Flavell, J. H. (1979). Metacognition and cognitive monitoring: A new area of cognitive-developmental inquiry. *American Psychologist, 34*(10), 906-911.

[3] Hamachek, 1995, as noted on page 342 of Schleiger, L. L. F., and Dull, R. B. (2009). Metacognition and performance in the accounting classroom. *Issues in Accounting Education, 24*(3), 339-367.

[4] Quotation from page 5 of Paris, S. G. and Winograd, P. (2003). *The role of self-regulated learning in contextual teaching: Principles and practices for teacher preparation.* A commissioned paper for the U.S. Department of Education project Preparing Teachers to Use Contextual Teaching and Learning Strategies To Improve Student Success In and Beyond School. Retrieved from: http://files.eric.ed.gov/fulltext/ED479905.pdf

[5] Quotation from page 16 of Grimes, P. W. (2002). The overconfident principles of economics student: An examination of a metacognitive skill. *Journal of Economic Education, 33*(1), 15-30.

[6] Schraw, G., and Dennison, R. S. (1994). Assessing metacognitive awareness. *Contemporary Educational Psychology, 19*(4), 460-475.

[7] Coutinho, S. A. (2007). The relationship between goals, metacognition, and academic success. *Educate~, 7*(1), 39-47.

[8] Efklides, A. (2011). Interactions of metacognition with motivation and affect in self-regulated learning: The MASRL model. *Educational Psychologist, 46*(1), 6-25.

[9] Paris, S. G. and Winograd, P. (2003). The role of self-regulated learning in contextual teaching: Principles and practices for teacher preparation. A commissioned paper for the U.S. Department of Education project Preparing Teachers to Use Contextual Teaching and Learning Strategies To Improve Student Success In and Beyond

School. Retrieved from: http://files.eric.ed.gov/fulltext/ED479905. pdf

[10] Efklides, A. (2008). Metacognition: Defining its facets and levels of functioning in relation to self-regulation and co-regulation. *European Psychologist, 13*(4), 277-287.

[11] Azevedo, R. (2005). Using hypermedia as a metacognitive tool for enhancing student learning? The role of self-regulated learning. *Educational Psychologist, 40*(4), 199-209.

[12] Pintrich, P. R. (2002). The role of metacognitive knowledge in learning, teaching, and assessing. *Theory Into Practice, 41*(4), 219-225.

[13] Kruger, J., and Dunning, D. (1999). Unskilled and unaware of it: how difficulties in recognizing one's own incompetence lead to inflated self-assessments. *Journal of Personality and Social Psychology, 77*(6), 1121-1134.

[14] Tanner, K. D. (2012). Promoting student metacognition. *CBE-Life Sciences Education, 11*(2), 113-120.

[15] Information and chart from page 120 of Schraw, G. (1998). Promoting general metacognitive awareness. *Instructional Science, 26*(1-2), 113-125.

[16] The ideas in this paragraph are related to insights offered in Efklides, A. (2011).

[17] Pintrich, P. R., and De Groot, E. V. (1990). Motivational and self-regulated learning components of classroom academic performance. *Journal of Educational Psychology, 82*(1), 33-40.

[18] Quotation from page 431 of McMahon, M., and Luca, J. (2001, December). Assessing students' self-regulatory skills. In *annual conference of the Australasian Society for Computers in Learning*

in Tertiary Education, Melbourne, Australia. (ERIC Document Reproduction Service No. ED467960).

Key #6: Self-regulated Learning

[1] Baumeister, R. F., Bratslavsky, E., Muraven, M., and Tice, D. M. (1998). Ego depletion: is the active self a limited resource? *Journal of Personality and Social Psychology, 74*(5), 1252-1265.

[2] Kennett, D. J., and Keefer, K. (2006). Impact of learned resourcefulness and theories of intelligence on academic achievement of university students: An integrated approach. *Educational Psychology, 26*(3), 441-457.

[3] When structure is provided as part of a scaffolded approach to learning, as suggested by Lev Vygotsky, it can facilitate learning. However, in this approach, structure and support is gradually removed as the student gains confidence and ability. My comment here is geared toward teachers who constantly give reminders, extend deadlines, threaten consequences, cajole, and otherwise provide extensive extrinsic motivators for students.

[4] Zimmerman, B. J. and Cleary, T. J. (2006). Adolescents' development of personal agency: The role of self-efficacy beliefs and self-regulatory skill. In F. Pajares and T. Urdan (Eds.), *Self-efficacy beliefs of adolescents* (pp. 45-70). Greenwich, CT: Information Age Publishing.

[5] Quotation from page 20 of Klassen, R. M. (2010). Confidence to manage learning: The self-efficacy for self-regulated learning of early adolescents with learning disabilities. *Learning Disability Quarterly, 33*, 19-30.

[6] Schraw, G., Crippen, K. J., and Hartley, K. (2006). Promoting self-regulation in science education: Metacognition as part of a

broader perspective on learning. *Research in Science Education, 36,* 111-139.

[7] For a review, see Puustinen, M., and Pulkkinen, L. (2001). Models of self-regulated learning: A review. *Scandinavian Journal of Educational Research, 45*(3), 269-286.

[8] Pintrich, P. R., and De Groot, E. V. (1990). Motivational and self-regulated learning components of classroom academic performance. *Journal of Educational Psychology, 82*(1), 33-40.

[9] Pintrich, P. R. (2004). A conceptual framework for assessing motivation and self-regulated learning in college students. *Educational Psychology Review, 16*(4), 385-407.

[10] Boekaerts, M., and Cascallar, E. (2006). How far have we moved toward the integration of theory and practice in self-regulation? *Educational Psychology Review, 18*(3), 199-210.

[11] Covington, M. V. (2000). Goal theory, motivation, and school achievement: An integrative review. *Annual Review of Psychology, 51*(1), 171-200.

[12] Risemberg, R., and Zimmerman, B. J. (1992). Self-regulated learning in gifted students. *Roeper Review, 15*(2), 98-101.

[13] Quotation from page 4 of Zimmerman, B. J. (1990). Self-regulated learning and academic achievement: An overview. *Educational Psychologist, 25*(1), 3-17.

[14] Paris, S. G. and Winograd, P. (2003). The role of self-regulated learning in contextual teaching: Principles and practices for teacher preparation. A commissioned paper for the U.S. Department of Education project Preparing Teachers to Use Contextual Teaching and Learning Strategies To Improve Student Success In and Beyond

School. Retrieved from: http://files.eric.ed.gov/fulltext/ED479905. pdf

[15] Cleary, T. J., and Zimmerman, B. J. (2004). Self-regulation empowerment program: A school-based program to enhance self-regulated and self-motivated cycles of student learning. *Psychology in the Schools, 41*(5), 537-550.

[16] Pajares, F. (2002). Gender and perceived self-efficacy in self-regulated learning. *Theory Into Practice, 41*(2), 116-125.

[17] Covington, M. V. (2000).

[18] Quotation from page 73 of Zimmerman, B. J. (1998). Academic studying and the development of personal skill: A self-regulatory perspective. *Educational Psychologist, 33*(2/3), 73-86.

[19] These are outlined in Zimmerman, B. J. (1994). Dimensions of academic self-regulation: A conceptual framework for education. In D. H. Schunk and B. J. Zimmerman (Eds.), *Self-regulation of learning and performance: Issues and educational applications* (pp. 3-21). Hilldale, NJ: Lawrence Erlbaum Associates.

[20] Miller, R. B., and Brickman, S. J. (2004). A model of future-oriented motivation and self-regulation. *Educational Psychology Review, 16*(1), 9-33.

[21] Miller, R. B., and Brickman, S. J. (2004).

[22] Sitzmann, T., and Ely, K. (2011). A meta-analysis of self-regulated learning in work-related training and educational attainment: what we know and where we need to go. *Psychological Bulletin, 137*(3), 421-442.

[23] Locke, E. A., and Latham, G. P. (2002). Building a practically useful theory of goal setting and task motivation. *American Psychologist, 57*(9), 705-717.

[24] Boekaerts, M., and Corno, L. (2005).

[25] Research by Ruvolo and Markus (1992) as cited in Valentine, J. C., DuBois, D. L., and Cooper, H. (2004). The relation between self-beliefs and academic achievement: A meta-analytic review. *Educational Psychologist, 39*(2), 111-133.

[26] Quotation from page 109 of Boekaerts, M. (1996). Self-regulated learning at the junction of cognition and motivation. *European Psychologist, 1*(2), 100-112.

[27] Puustinen, M., and Pulkkinen, L. (2001).

[28] Sitzmann, T., and Ely, K. (2011).

[29] Eccles, J. (1983). Expectancies, values and academic behaviors. In J. T. Spence (Ed.), *Achievement and Achievement Motives* (pp. 75-146). San Francisco: Freeman.

[30] Pintrich, P. R., and De Groot, E. V. (1990).

[31] Wolters, C. A. (2003).

[32] Renninger, K. A., and Hidi, S. (2011). Revisiting the conceptualization, measurement, and generation of interest. *Educational Psychologist, 46*(3), 168-184.

[33] Boekaerts, M. (1996).

[34] Boekaerts, M., and Corno, L. (2005).

[35] Quotation from page 7 of Zimmerman, B. J. (1990).

[36] Pintrich, P. R. (2003). A motivational science perspective on the role of student motivation in learning and teaching contexts. *Journal of Educational Psychology, 95*(4), 667-686.

[37] Quotation from page 428 of Collier, P. J., and Morgan, D. L. (2008). Is that paper really due today? Differences in first-generation and traditional college students' understanding of faculty expectations. *Higher Education, 55*(4), 425-446.

[38] Acher, J., and Scevak, J. J. (1998). Enhancing students' motivation to learn: Achievement goals in university classrooms. *Educational Psychology, 18*(2), 205-223.

[39] Quotation from page 53 of Zimmerman, B. J. and Cleary, T. J. (2006).

[40] Topping, K. (1998). Peer assessment between students in colleges and universities. *Review of Educational Research, 68*(3), 249-276.

[41] Zimmerman, B. J., and Martinez-Pons, M. (1988). Construct validation of a strategy model of student self-regulated learning. *Journal of Educational Psychology, 80*(3), 284-290.

[42] Zimmerman, B. J. (1998).

[43] Pintrich, P. R. (2004).

[44] Schunk, D. H. (2005). Self-regulated learning: The educational legacy of Paul R. Pintrich. *Educational Psychologist, 40*(2), 85-94.

[45] Azevedo, R. (2005). Using hypermedia as a metacognitive tool for enhancing student learning? The role of self-regulated learning. *Educational Psychologist, 40*(4), 199-209.

[46] Quotation from page 60 of Zimmerman, B. J. and Cleary, T. J. (2006).

[47] Azevedo, R. (2005).

[48] Quotation from page 202 of Azevedo, R. (2005).

Key #7: Avoiding Thinking Errors

[1] Crosby, R. A., and Yarber, W. L. (2001). Perceived versus actual knowledge about correct condom use among US adolescents: results from a national study. *Journal of Adolescent Health, 28*(5), 415-420.

[2] Risucci, D. A., Tortolani, A. J., and Ward, R. J. (1989). Ratings of surgical residents by self, supervisors and peers. *Surgery, Gynecology & Obstetrics, 169*(6), 519-526.

[3] Bol, L., and Hacker, D. J. (2001). A comparison of the effects of practice tests and traditional review on performance and calibration. *The Journal of Experimental Education, 69*(2), 133-151.

[4] Fischhoff, B., Slovic, P., and Lichtenstein, S. (1977). Knowing with certainty: The appropriateness of extreme confidence. *Journal of Experimental Psychology: Human Perception and Performance, 3*(4), 552-564.

[5] Quotation from page 70 of Bjork, R. A. (1999). Assessing our own competence: Heuristics and illusions. In D. Gopher and A. Koriat (Eds.), *Attention and performance XVII: Cognitive regulation of performance: Interaction of theory and application* (pp. 435-459). Cambridge, MA: MIT Press.

[6] Quotation from page 1121 of Kruger, J., and Dunning, D. (1999). Unskilled and unaware of it: how difficulties in recognizing one's own incompetence lead to inflated self-assessments. *Journal of Personality and Social Psychology, 77*(6), 1121-1134.

[7] Sheldon, O. J., Dunning, D., and Ames, D. R. (2014). Emotionally unskilled, unaware, and uninterested in learning more: Reactions to feedback about deficits in emotional intelligence. *Journal of Applied Psychology, 99*(1), 1-13.

[8] Carter, T. J., and Dunning, D. (2008). Faulty Self-Assessment: Why evaluating one's own competence is an intrinsically difficult task. *Social and Personality Psychology Compass, 2*(1), 346-360.

[9] Shaw III, J. S. (1996). Increases in eyewitness confidence resulting from postevent questioning. *Journal of Experimental Psychology Applied, 2*(2), 126-146.

[10] Chemers, M. M., Hu, L. T., and Garcia, B. F. (2001). Academic self-efficacy and first year college student performance and adjustment. *Journal of Educational Psychology, 93*(1), 55-64.

[11] The survey was reported in Dunning, D., Heath, C., and Suls, J. M. (2004). Flawed self-assessment: Implications for health, education, and the workplace. *Psychological Science in the Public Interest, 5*(3), 69-106.

[12] Karpicke, J. D., Butler, A. C., and Roediger III, H. L. (2009). Metacognitive strategies in student learning: Do students practise retrieval when they study on their own? *Memory, 17*(4), 471-479.

[13] Dunning, D., Johnson, K., Ehrlinger, J., and Kruger, J. (2003). Why people fail to recognize their own incompetence. *Current Directions in Psychological Science, 12*(3), 83-87.

[14] Svanum, S., and Bigatti, S. (2006). Grade expectations: Informed or uninformed optimism, or both? *Teaching of Psychology, 33*(1), 14-18.

[15] Sinkavich, F. J. (1995). Performance and metamemory: Do students know what they don't know? *Journal of Instructional Psychology, 22*, 77-87.

[16] Hacker, D. J., Bol, L., Horgan, D. D., and Rakow, E. A. (2000). Test prediction and performance in a classroom context. *Journal of Educational Psychology,92*(1), 160-170.

[17] Pintrich, P. R. (2003). A motivational science perspective on the role of student motivation in learning and teaching contexts. *Journal of Educational Psychology, 95*(4), 667-686.

[18] Schwartz, D. L., Chase, C. C., & Bransford, J. D. (2012). Resisting overzealous transfer: Coordinating previously successful routines with needs for new learning. *Educational Psychologist, 47*(3), 204-214.

[19] Caputo, D., and Dunning, D. (2005). What you don't know: The role played by errors of omission in imperfect self-assessments. *Journal of Experimental Social Psychology, 41*(5), 488-505.

[20] Dunning, D., Heath, C., and Suls, J. M. (2004).

[21] Carter, T. J., and Dunning, D. (2008).

[22] Carter, T. J., and Dunning, D. (2008).

[23] Dunning, D., Heath, C., and Suls, J. M. (2004).

[24] Bjork, R. A. (1999).

[25] Dunning, D., Heath, C., and Suls, J. M. (2004).

[26] Dunning, D., Heath, C., and Suls, J. M. (2004).

[27] Dunlosky, J., and Hertzog, C. (1998). Training programs to improve learning in later adulthood: Helping older adults educate themselves. In D. J. Hacker, J. Dunlosky, and A. C. Graesser (Eds.), *Metacognition in Educational Theory and Practice (pp. 249-275)*. Mahwah, NJ: Erlbaum.

[28] Thiede, K. W., and Dunlosky, J. (1999). Toward a general model of self-regulated study: An analysis of selection of items for study and self-paced study time. *Journal of Experimental Psychology: Learning, Memory, and Cognition, 25*(4), 1024-1037.

[29] Son, L. K., and Metcalfe, J. (2000). Metacognitive and control strategies in study-time allocation. *Journal of Experimental Psychology: Learning, Memory, and Cognition, 26*(1), 204-221.

[30] Buehler, R., Griffin, D., and Ross, M. (2002). Inside the planning fallacy: The causes and consequences of optimistic time predictions. In T. Gilovich, D. Griffin, and D. Kahneman (Eds.), *Heuristics and biases: The psychology of intuitive judgment* (pp. 251-270). Cambridge, England: Cambridge University Press.

[31] Quotation from page 77 of Dunning, D., Heath, C., and Suls, J. M. (2004).

[32] Dunning, D., Heath, C., and Suls, J. M. (2004).

[33] Pintrich, P. R. (2003).

[34] Carter, T. J., and Dunning, D. (2008).

[35] Pintrich, P. R. (2003).

[36] Hassel, H., and Lourey, J. (2005). The dea(r)th of student responsibility. *College Teaching, 53*(1), 2-13.

[37] Langer, E. J. (1975). The illusion of control. *Journal of Personality and Social Psychology, 32*(2), 311-328.

Culture – The Thinking Skills Keychain

[1] Masuda, T. and Nisbett, R. E. (2001). Attending holistically versus analytically: Comparing the context sensitivity of Japanese and Americans. *Journal of Personality and Social Psychology, 81*(5), 922-934.

[2] Quotation from page 863 of De Castella, K., Byrne, D., and Covington, M. (2013). Unmotivated or motivated to fail? A cross-cultural study

of achievement motivation, fear of failure, and student disengagement. *Journal of Educational Psychology, 105*(3), 861-880.

[3] Stephens, N. M., Fryberg, S. A., Markus, H. R., Johnson, C. S., and Covarrubias, R. (2012). Unseen disadvantage: how American universities' focus on independence undermines the academic performance of first-generation college students. *Journal of Personality and Social Psychology, 102*(6), 1178.

[4] Quotation from page 463 of Myers, D. G. (2014). *Exploring Psychology* (9th ed.). New York, NY: Worth.

[5] Greene, T. G., Marti, C. N., and McClenney, K. (2008). The effort–outcome gap: Differences for African American and Hispanic community college students in student engagement and academic achievement. *The Journal of Higher Education, 79*(5), 513-539.

[6] Nisbett, R. E., Peng, K., Choi, I., and Norenzayan, A. (2001). Culture and systems of thought: holistic versus analytic cognition. *Psychological Review, 108*(2), 291.

[7] Fyans, L. J., Salili, F., Maehr, M. L., and Desai, K. A. (1983). A cross-cultural exploration into the meaning of achievement. *Journal of Personality and Social Psychology, 44*(5), 1000-1013.

[8] Quotations from pages 230-231 of Markus, H. R., and Kitayama, S. (1991).

[9] Cruce, T. M., Wolniak, G. C., Seifert, T. A., and Pascarella, E. T. (2006). Impacts of good practices on cognitive development, learning orientations, and graduate degree plans during the first year of college. *Journal of College Student Development, 47*(4), 365-383.

[10] Carson, L. R. (2009). "I am because we are:" Collectivism as a foundational characteristic of African American college student identity

and academic achievement. *Social Psychology of Education, 12*(3), 327-344.

[11] For example, see Nisbett, R. E., Peng, K., Choi, I., and Norenzayan, A. (2001).

[12] Markus, H. R., and Kitayama, S. (1991). Culture and the self: Implications for cognition, emotion, and motivation. *Psychological Review, 98*(2), 224-253.

[13] Heine, S. J., Kitayama, S., Lehman, D. R., Takata, T., Ide, E., Leung, C., and Matsumoto, H. (2001). Divergent consequences of success and failure in Japan and North America: An investigation of self-improving motivations and malleable selves. *Journal of Personality and Social Psychology, 81*(4), 599–615.

[14] Majer, J. M. (2009). Self-efficacy and academic success among ethnically diverse first-generation community college students. *Journal of Diversity in Higher Education, 2*(4), 243-250.

[15] Núñez, A. M., Sparks, P. J., and Hernández, E. A. (2011). Latino access to community colleges and Hispanic-serving institutions: A national study. *Journal of Hispanic Higher Education, 10*(1), 18-40.

[16] Quotation from page 459 of Plaut, V. C., and Markus, H. R. (2005). The "inside" story. A cultural-historical analysis of being smart and motivated, American style. In Andrew Elliot and Carol Dweck (Eds). *Handbook of Competence and Motivation.* (pp.457-488). New York: Guilford.

[17] Plaut, V. C., and Markus, H. R. (2005).

Powerful Learning Strategies

[1] Gurung, R. A. R., Weidert, J., and Jeske, A. (2010). Focusing on how students study. *Journal of the Scholarship of Teaching and Learning, 10(1)*, 28-35.

[2] Quotation from page 442 of Daley, B. J., and Torre, D. M. (2010). Concept maps in medical education: An analytical literature review. *Medical Education, 44*, 440-448.

[3] Weinstein, C. E., Acee, T. W., and Jung, J. (2011). Self-regulation and learning strategies. *New Directions for Teaching and Learning, 126*, 45-53.

[4] Gurung, R. A. R., et. al. (2010).

[5] Simsek, A., & Balaban, J. (2010). Learning Strategies of Successful and Unsuccessful University Students. *Online Submission, 1(1)*, 36-45.

[6] Weinstein, C. E., et. al. (2011).

[7] Miller, G. (1956). The magical number seven, plus or minus two: Some limits on our capacity for processing information. *Psychological Review, 63*, 81-97.

[8] Miller, G. (1956).

[9] Quotation from page 115 of Storm, B. C., Friedman, M. C., Murayama, K., and Bjork, R. A. (2014). On the transfer of prior tests or study events to subsequent study. *Journal of Experimental Psychology: Learning, Memory, and Cognition, 40(1)*, 115-124.

[10] Dunlosky, J., and Rawson, K. A. (2015). Practice tests, spaced practice, and successive relearning: Tips for classroom use and for guiding students' learning. *Scholarship of Teaching and Learning in Psychology, 1(1)*, 72-78.

[11] Storm, B. C., et. al. (2014).

[12] See Littrell-Baez, M. K., Friend, A., Caccamise, D., and Okochi, C. (2015). Using retrieval practice and metacognitive skills to improve content learning. *Journal of Adolescent & Adult Literacy, 58(8),* 682-689.

[13] Pavlik, P. I., Jr., and Anderson, J. R. (2005). Practice and forgetting effects on vocabulary memory: An activation-based model of the spacing effect. *Cognitive Science, 29(4),* 559-586.

[14] Roediger III, H. L., Putnam, A. L., and Smith, M. A. (2011). Ten benefits of testing and their applications to educational practice. *Psychology of Learning and Motivation-Advances in Research and Theory, 55,* 1-36.

[15] Dunlosky, J. (2013). Strengthening the student toolbox: Study strategies to boost learning. *American Educator, Fall 2013,* 12-21.

[16] Gurung, R. A. R. (2005). How do students really study (and does it matter)? *Teaching of Psychology, 32(4),* 238-240.

[17] Quotation from page 97 of Lyle, K. B., and Crawford, N. A. (2011). Retrieving essential material at the end of lectures improves performance on statistics exams. *Teaching of Psychology, 38(2),* 94-97.

[18] Thalheimer, W. (2003). The learning benefits of questions. Retrieved June 17, 2016, from http://www.work-learning.com/ma/PP_WP003.asp

[19] Debb, S. M., and Debb, S. M. (2012). Teaching introductory psychology in the community college classroom: Enhancing student understanding and retention of essential information. *Inquiry, 17(1),* 27-36.

[20] Cepeda, N. J., Pashler, H., Vul, E., Wixted, J. T., and Rohrer, D. (2006). Distributed practice in verbal recall tasks: A review and quantitative synthesis. *Psychological bulletin*, *132(3)*, 354.

[21] Quotation from page 79 of Dunlosky, J., and Rawson, K. A. (2015).

[22] Dunlosky, J., and Rawson, K. A. (2015).

[23] Rawson, K. A., and Dunlosky, J. (2013). Relearning attenuates the benefits and costs of spacing. *Journal of Experimental Psychology: General*, *142(4)*, 1113-1129.

[24] Weinstein, C. E., Acee, T. W., and Jung, J. (2011).

[25] Kornell, N., and Bjork, R. A. (2008). Optimising self-regulated study: The benefits—and costs—of dropping flashcards. *Memory*, *16*(2), 125-136.

[26] Bloom, B. S., Engelhart, M. D., Furst, E. J., Hill, W. H., and Krathwohl, D. R. (1956). *Taxonomy of educational objectives: The classification of educational goals. Handbook I: Cognitive domain*. New York: David McKay.

[27] Quotation from page 350 of Cannon, H. M., and Feinstein, A. H. (2014). Bloom beyond Bloom: Using the revised taxonomy to develop experiential learning strategies. *Developments in Business Simulation and Experiential Learning*, *32*, 348-356.

[28] Anderson, L. W., Krathwohl, D. R., and Bloom, B. S. (2001). *A taxonomy for learning, teaching, and assessing: A revision of Bloom's taxonomy of educational objectives*. Allyn & Bacon.

[29] Debb, S. M., and Debb, S. M. (2012).

[30] Crowe, A., Dirks, C., and Wenderoth, M. P. (2008). Biology in bloom: implementing Bloom's taxonomy to enhance student learning in biology. *CBE-Life Sciences Education*, *7(4)*, 368-381.

[31] Berry, J. W., and Chew, S. L. (2008). Improving learning through interventions of student-generated questions and concept maps. *Teaching of Psychology, 35(4)*, 305-312.

[32] Craik, F. I. (2002). Levels of processing: Past, present…and future? *Memory, 10(5-6)*, 305-318.

[33] Quotation from page 1176 of Irvine, L. M. C. (1995). Can concept mapping be used to promote meaningful learning in nurse education? *Journal of Advanced Nursing, 21*, 1175-1179.

[34] Chen, B., Hirumi, A., and Zhang, N. J. (2007). Investigating the use of advance organizers as an instructional strategy for web-based distance education. *The Quarterly Review of Distance Education, 8(3)*, 223-231.

[35] Ausubel, D. P. (1968). Educational psychology: A cognitive view. New York: Holt, Rinehart, & Winston.

[36] Kovalik, C. L., and Williams, M. A. (2011). Cartoons as advance organizers. *Journal of Visual Literacy, 30(2)*, 40-64.

[37] Nestojko, J. F., Bui, D. C., Kornell, N., & Bjork, E. L. (2014). Expecting to teach enhances learning and organization of knowledge in free recall of text passages. *Memory & cognition, 42(7)*, 1038-1048.

[38] Petty, T. (2014). Motivating first-generation students to academic success and college completion. *College Student Journal, 48(2)*, 257-264.

[39] Macan, T. H., Shahani, C., Dipboye, R. L., & Phillips, A. P. (1990). College students' time management: Correlations with academic performance and stress. *Journal of Educational Psychology, 82(4)*, 760-768.

[40] Covey, S. R. (1989). The 7 habits of highly effective people. New York.

[41] Sanbonmatsu, D. M., Strayer, D. L., Medeiros-Ward, N., & Watson, J. M. (2013). Who multi-tasks and why? Multi-tasking ability, perceived multi-tasking ability, impulsivity, and sensation seeking. *PloS one, 8*(1), e54402.

[42] Kahneman, D. (1973). Attention and effort. Englewood Cliffs, NJ: Prentice-Hall.

[43] Ophir, E., Nass, C., & Wagner, A. D. (2009). Cognitive control in media multitaskers. *Proceedings of the National Academy of Sciences, 106*(37), 15583-15587.

[44] Watson, J. M., & Strayer, D. L. (2010). Supertaskers: Profiles in extraordinary multitasking ability. *Psychonomic Bulletin & Review, 17*(4), 479-485.

[45] Misra, R., & McKean, M. (2000). College students' academic stress and its relation to their anxiety, time management, and leisure satisfaction. *American Journal of Health Studies, 16*(1), 41-51.

[46] Krumrei-Mancuso, E. J., Newton, F. B., Kim, E., & Wilcox, D. (2013). Psychosocial factors predicting first-year college student success. *Journal of College Student Development, 54*(3), 247-266.

Personal Growth and Success

[1] Thomas, R. (1996). Long day. On Yourself or someone like you [CD]. Atlanta: Lava Records.

[2] Salovey, P., & Mayer, J. D. (1990). Emotional intelligence. *Imagination, Cognition and Personality, 9*(3), 185-211.

[3] Goleman, D. (1995). Emotional intelligence: Why it can matter more than IQ. New York: Bantam Books.

[4] Puri, P., Kaur, T., & Yadav, K. (2016). Emotional intelligence and stress among college students. *Indian Journal of Health and Wellbeing, 7*(3), 334-336.

[5] Garg, R., Levin, E., & Tremblay, L. (2016). Emotional intelligence: impact on post-secondary academic achievement. *Social Psychology of Education, 19*(3), 627-642.

[6] Brackett, M. A., Rivers, S. E., Reyes, M. R., & Salovey, P. (2012). Enhancing academic performance and social and emotional competence with the RULER feeling words curriculum. *Learning and Individual Differences, 22*(2), 218-224.

[7] Gardner, H. (1993). Frames of mind: The theory of multiple intelligences. New York, NY: BasicBooks.

[8] Gardner, H. (1995). Reflections on multiple intelligences: Myths and messages. *Phi Delta Kappan, 77*, 200-209.

[9] Lujan, H. L., & DiCarlo, S. E. (2006). First-year medical students prefer multiple learning styles. *Advances in Physiology Education, 30*(1), 13-16.

[10] Prochaska, J. O., & DiClemente, C. C. (2005). The transtheoretical approach. In J. C. Norcross & M. R. Goldfried (Eds.), Handbook of psychotherapy integration (147-171). New York: Oxford University Press.

[11] Norcross, J. C., Krebs, P. M., & Prochaska, J. O. (2011). Stages of change. *Journal of Clinical Psychology, 67*(2), 143-154.

[12] Prochaska, J. O., Norcross, J. C., & DiClemente, C. C. (1995). Changing for good. New York: Avon Books.

[13] Epstein, R. (2011). Fight the frazzled mind. *Scientific American Mind, 22*(4), 30-35.

[14] Greenberg, M. (2017). The Stress-proof brain: Master your emotional response to stress using mindfulness and neuroplasticity. Oakland, CA: New Harbinger Publications.

[15] Gonzales, L. (2014). Flight 232: A story of disaster and survival. New York: W. W. Norton & Company.

[16] Durlak, J. A., Weissberg, R. P., Dymnicki, A. B., Taylor, R. D., & Schellinger, K. B. (2011). The impact of enhancing students' social and emotional learning: A meta-analysis of school-based universal interventions. *Child Development, 82*(1), 405-432.